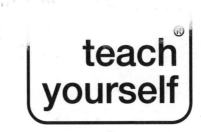

teach®
yourself

chess

®

teach
yourself

chess
william hartston

For over 60 years, more than
40 million people have learnt over
750 subjects the **teach yourself**
way, with impressive results.

be where you want to be
with **teach yourself**

For UK order enquiries: please contact Bookpoint Ltd, 130 Milton Park, Abingdon, Oxon OX14 4SB. Telephone: +44 (0) 1235 827720. Fax: +44 (0) 1235 400454. Lines are open from 09.00–18.00, Monday to Saturday, with a 24-hour message answering service. Details about our titles and how to order are available on our website: www.teachyourself.co.uk

For USA order enquiries: please contact McGraw-Hill Customer Services, PO Box 545, Blacklick, OH 43004-0545, USA. Telephone: 1-800-722-4726. Fax: 1-614-755-5645.

For Canada order enquiries: please contact McGraw-Hill Ryerson Ltd, 300 Water St, Whitby, Ontario L1N 9B6, Canada. Telephone: 905 430 5000. Fax: 905 430 5020.

Long renowned as the authoritative source for self-guided learning – with more than 30 million copies sold worldwide – the *Teach Yourself* series includes over 300 titles in the fields of languages, crafts, hobbies, business, computing and education.

British Library Cataloguing in Publication Data: a catalogue record for this title is available from The British Library.

Library of Congress Catalog Card Number: on file.

First published in UK 1996 by Hodder Headline Ltd, 338 Euston Road, London, NW1 3BH.

First published in US 1996 by Contemporary Books, a Division of the McGraw-Hill Companies, 1 Prudential Plaza, 130 East Randolph Street, Chicago, IL 60601 USA.

This edition published 2003.

The 'Teach Yourself' name and logo are registered trade marks of Hodder & Stoughton Ltd.

Typeset by Transet Limited, Coventry, England.
Printed in Great Britain for Hodder & Stoughton Educational, a division of Hodder Headline Ltd, 338 Euston Road, London NW1 3BH by Cox & Wyman Ltd, Reading, Berkshire.

Papers used in this book are natural, renewable and recyclable products. They are made from wood grown in sustainable forests. The logging and manufacturing processes conform to the environmental regulations of the country of origin.

Impression number   10 9 8 7 6 5 4 3
Year   2009 2008 2007 2006 2005 2004 2003

contents

introduction

... a battle without armour, a war without blood, and as elaborate a waste of human intelligence as you could find anywhere outside an advertising agency.
Raymond Chandler, The Long Goodbye, 1953

When author Raymond Chandler wanted to give his detective, Philip Marlowe, a hobby, it was quite natural that he settled on chess. The game has been around for at least 1400 years, with its rules largely unchanged for half a millennium, and its long history has ensured its pre-eminent place among intellectual board games.

Too serious to be dismissed as merely a game, chess has a logic that appeals to scientists and mathematicians, and a beauty that may attract the artist in all of us. Most beguiling of all, however, is the lucky accident of the game's inherent difficulty. However much we may study it, perfect chess will always remain just beyond the intellectual capabilities of even the best of us. Yet the very best will manage to get so close that perfection seems tantalizingly almost within their grasp.

Criticized by kings as subversive, praised by politicians as character-forming, condemned by clerics as time-wasting and distracting, the game of chess has survived all man's attempts to conquer it or suppress it. The International Chess Federation now claims more member countries than the governing body for any comparable sporting or leisure activity, other than the footballers of FIFA or the athletes of the IAAF.

You may play competitively or just for fun; you may even – as Philip Marlowe apparently preferred – not play at all, but relish the solitary pleasure of eavesdropping on the thoughts of the great masters as you play through their games. Whatever your chess ambitions, you will surely find that the greater your understanding of the game, the more you will enjoy it.

This book is intended as the first steps on that journey of understanding. Starting with the basic rules of the game and elementary tactics (Chapters 01–04), we move on to a discussion of strategy and planning, showing how simple ideas can be combined to produce concepts of great beauty and cunning. The chapters on Openings and Endgames are designed to equip the reader with the techniques needed in competitive play, while the Illustrative Games (Chapter 08) will, I hope, give a feeling of the way the greatest players can combine logic and imagination to create effects that can even lift the spirit of a cynical fictional detective.

The essentially timeless nature of the game of chess has meant that few changes have been necessary since I wrote the first edition of this book in 1985. In two areas, however, advances in technology have made chess even more accessible to many. First, rapid improvements in computers have ensured that programs of almost Grandmaster strength are now available for all. Second, the rapid growth of the World Wide Web has provided a way for any person with Internet access to keep up with chess news, follow many major events live, and find an opponent for a friendly game without going out of their front door. For those who wish to explore these opportunities, I have therefore added a brief section on chess in the twenty-first century.

William Hartston
London 2002

01

the rules of the game

In this chapter you will learn:
- the basic moves of the pieces, check, checkmate and stalemate
- special rules such as castling, pawn promotion, en passant capture, and the various ways a game can end in a draw
- the essential laws of chess, and how to write down the moves of a game.

The first diagram shows the chessmen set up for the beginning of a game of chess. One player sits behind the white men and conducts their operations; his opponent faces him across the board, deciding the moves for the black pieces.

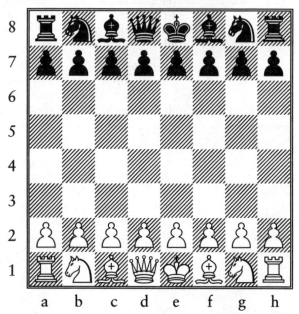

Each of the different chess pieces has its own individual mode of moving. Much of the charm and beauty, and indeed much of the difficulty, of the game of chess lies in the manner of the cooperation and conflict between pieces with distinct patterns of movement. This opening chapter explains the moves of the pieces and the other rules of the game. Later we shall see how the relative values of different pieces can vary according to the circumstances of the other men on the board.

Before proceeding with the pieces, we must begin with a brief word about the board itself. This consists of sixty-four squares, in an eight-by-eight array, the squares coloured alternately light and dark, referred to respectively as the white squares and black squares. The board is always set out with a white square on the right-hand corner of each player. The white pieces at the start of the game occupy the back rows. From left to right, along the back row, Rook, Knight, Bishop, Queen, King, Bishop, Knight, Rook, with the eight Pawns filling the row in front of them. The rear line of black pieces are the same as their white counterparts directly facing them. Each Queen thus begins the game on a square of her own colour: White's Queen on the left of her King, Black's on the right of her King.

The players make their moves alternately, White beginning the game. A move involves the transference of a piece from one square to another. No player may make two consecutive moves, neither may a player 'pass' when it is his turn to move.

Most of the chess pieces move in straight lines and their powers are simply grasped. There are three important and obvious types of straight line on the board: the *files* running up and down the board; the *ranks* running side to side; and the *diagonals*, lines of squares of the same colour, running at 45° angles to the ranks and files.

The ranks and files provide a convenient coordinate system for describing the chess moves. Each square on the board lies on one of the eight ranks and one of the eight files. The ranks are numbered from 1 to 8 beginning at White's side of the board; the files are lettered from a to h, left to right as viewed by White. Thus each square may be uniquely identified by a letter-number pair. We shall see how this is used in chess notation at the end of this chapter.

Moves of the pieces

The Rook

The ranks and files are the domain of the Rook, which can move as far as desired across empty squares up, down or across the board in a straight line. On an empty board a Rook, whatever square it is on, thus has a choice of fourteen squares to which it may move: seven on the vertical line of squares through its own square, seven on the horizontal line.

The Bishop

Bishops traverse the board along the diagonals, and may travel as far as they like along squares of the same colour. As with the Rook, the Bishop may only travel over empty spaces; if its path is impeded by the presence of another piece, it cannot 'jump over'. Each Bishop can never leave the squares of the colour on which it began the game.

The diagram shows the moves of Rook and Bishop. Each may travel to any square shown on the path of the arrows through it. As can be seen, a Bishop in the middle of the board has the choice of up to 13 squares, whereas one in the corner only has seven possible moves.

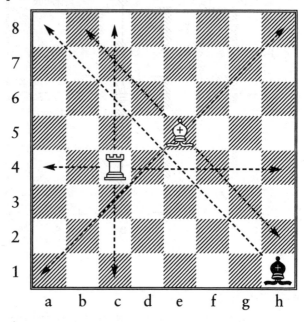

The Queen

The Queen is the most powerful piece on the board. She can move in straight lines along ranks, files or diagonals, so from any square she combines the possible moves of the Rook with those of the Bishop.

The King

The two Kings have a special role in the game, since the object of the game, as laid down in the rules, is the pursuit and capture of the enemy King. We shall come to that in a moment; for the time being, it is only necessary to know that the kKing has the shortest move of all – just one square in any direction.

The diagram opposite illustrates the moves of King and Queen. In the centre of the board the Queen commands 27 squares. The King never has more than eight.

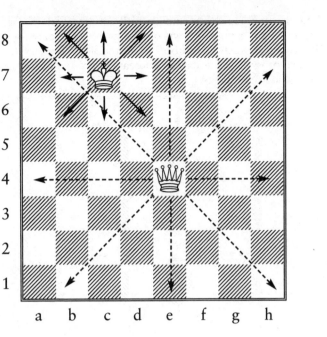

The Knight

There are many, perhaps too many, ways to describe the move of the Knight, the only chess piece which appears not to move in straight lines. His is a two-square move, bisecting the path of Rook and Bishop. In the diagram overleaf it is illustrated as one square like a Rook followed by a square in the manner of a Bishop, still moving away from the square of the original departure. Some prefer to think of the Knight's move as two squares vertically followed by one to the side, or two to the side and one up or down. However one chooses to describe it, the Knight's move is more easily visualized than explained. It should be mastered without difficulty, and with practice will come to be viewed as a single move from square to square, rather than a combination move involving change of direction.

The diagram illustrates the eight possible Knight moves from a centre square. The white Knight may move to any of the squares indicated by the arrow-tips. Note that the Black Knight in the corner has its possible moves reduced to two.

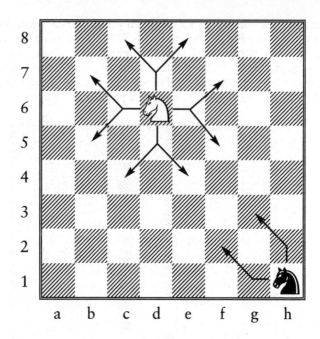

Unlike Rook, Bishop and Queen, the Knight cannot be impeded by other men in its path. The Knight gives the impression of being able to 'jump over' pieces, though one might equally well say that it can move between them. Whereas Rook, Bishop and Queen may be viewed as having lines of action along which they can move as far as desired, the Knight, like the King, has only a limited length of move. Rook, Bishop or Queen can reach any square on an empty board from any other in not more than two moves (provided the square is the appropriate colour in the case of the Bishop). A Knight can take as many as six moves to make a desired journey between two squares.

Capturing

Capturing enemy pieces

If an enemy man stands on a square to which a piece could otherwise move, that man may be captured. The capture is effected by removing the man to be captured from the board and placing the capturing piece on the square on which the captured piece stood. In the diagram position, the White Rook can capture the Black Bishop, if it is White's move, or the Black Bishop could capture the White Knight, if it is Black to move. Note that Black's Bishop blocks the Rook's line of action, preventing its movement to the last two squares up the board, just as the White Knight hampers its progress sideways.

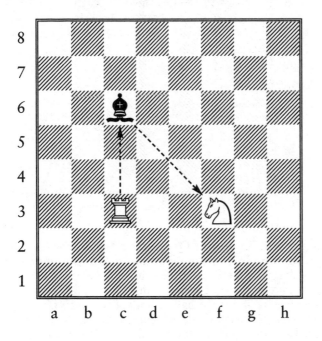

In chess, capturing is optional. If White chooses to capture the Bishop with his Rook, he simply removes the Bishop, replacing it with the Rook. Equally he may prefer to move the Rook or any other piece as he chooses, with or without a capture. The King is the only piece which may not be captured, for loss of the King signifies the end of the game. Attacks on the King will be discussed below. Whereas Rook, Knight, Bishop, Queen and King may in general capture anything along their lines of action (the King may make captures just as any other piece; the need to protect him from capture does not preclude his taking part in the carnage), the Pawn has special rules for its capturing moves. The Pawn is, in fact, exceptional in many ways, which we now explain.

The Pawn

The normal move of the Pawn is simple: it plods just one square forwards at a time. It alone of the chess pieces may never move backwards. On its *first* move, however, the Pawn may, if desired, be moved two squares forward instead of just one. That privilege is accorded to each of the eight Pawns on either side, but a Pawn may only advance two squares if both those squares are unoccupied, and the Pawn has not previously been moved.

As distinct from its forward mode of travel, the Pawn *captures* diagonally, but again only one square. It may not capture straight-forwards.

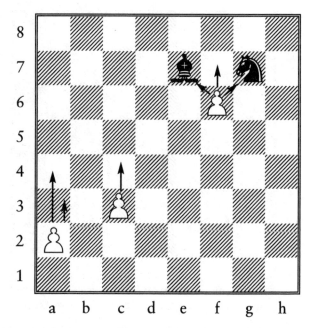

White's legal Pawn moves in the above diagram position are to any of the squares indicated by the arrows. The Black Bishop or Black Knight may be captured in the usual way, by removing the black piece from the board and replacing it with the capturing Pawn.

There are two further special rules involving Pawns. The first is their ability to promote. If a Pawn succeeds in making its way the full length of the board, arriving finally on the opponent's back line, then it may be promoted into any piece of the same colour other than a King. So if a White Pawn reaches the end of the board, it is removed and replaced by Queen, Rook, Knight or Bishop at the discretion of the White player. Promotion takes place immediately the Pawn reaches the end square; it cannot remain a Pawn. Usually the promoted Pawn is turned into a Queen, but as we shall see later there are circumstances where an apparently lesser piece may be preferable.

The final special rule for Pawns is the **en passant** capture, often improperly learned by beginners, but not really complicated. The diagram shows a typical situation in which the en passant rule may apply.

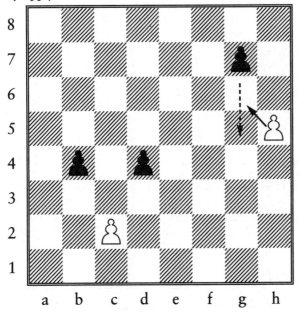

Any Pawn which advances two squares in a single move, passing over a square on which it could have been captured by an enemy Pawn, may still be captured by an enemy Pawn on that square just as if it had only advanced a single square. Thus, if the Black Pawn in the diagram position advances two squares, it may be captured by White's Pawn as indicated by the arrow. Black's Pawn is removed from the board and White's is moved to the empty square over which it passed. Equally, if the other White Pawn were to advance two squares, it could be captured in exactly the same fashion by either of the neighbouring Black Pawns.

The privilege of capturing en passant is only extended for the single move following the two-square advance of an enemy Pawn. As with other captures, the en passant Pawn capture is optional (except, of course, in the rare case of no other legal move being available), but the option expires as soon as another move is played on the board. If an en passant capture is not made as soon as the opportunity is created, then the Pawn may never be captured en passant at all. Only Pawns may capture, or be captured, en passant. And the capture may only take place immediately after a two-square advance of the Pawn to be captured.

As we shall see later, the special abilities of the Pawn to promote, and to a lesser extent to capture en passant, play a significant role towards the end of well-contested games when the heavier pieces may have vanished from the board by exchanges and the emphasis shifts from direct attacks to the careful nurturing of the Pawns in their journeys in search of promotion.

We are almost at the end of this explanation of the moves of the pieces, but there is just one more exceptional move to consider.

Castling

As we have seen, a normal move consists of a player taking one of his own pieces and changing its square on the board, with or without the capture of an enemy piece. There is just one exception to this rule: a double move of King and Rook known as **castling**. The privilege of castling is a method to enable the King to escape from the centre of the board, and for the Rook to come closer to the middle. Castling may take place only between a King and a Rook both still unmoved on the squares upon which they began the game.

Castling is effected by moving the King two squares along the back rank towards the Rook, then placing the Rook on the square over which the King has passed. The diagram on the next page indicates the situation of King and Rook after castling. Castling may take place with either Rook; in each case, the King moves two squares and the Rook apparently 'jumps over' the King. In the diagram, White has castled with his Rook on the King's side of the board, Black with the Rook on his Queen's side. (The two halves of the board are often referred to as 'King's side' and 'Queen's side' or K-side and Q-side for short.

Castling in each direction is often termed *castling long* – on the Q-side – or *castling short* – on the K-side.)

Castling may only be executed if the following conditions apply:

1 Neither the King nor the Rook taking part in the castling procedure has yet moved in the game.
2 The square upon which the King stands, the one over which it will pass, and the square upon which it will land must none of them be under attack from a hostile piece.

Note that this second condition only refers to the King; it does not matter if the Rook is under attack or, in the case of Q-side castling, if it passes over an attacked square. Thus in the position overleaf, White may castle, since his King does not pass over any threatened square (though his Rook does). Black may not castle on either side: on the short side, his King would land on an attacked square; on the long side, his King would have to pass over an attacked square.

In practice, castling is best executed by moving the King first, then the Rook. If the King moves first, there can be no ambiguity of intention and no suggestion that only the Rook move was intended. (Theoretically, of course, castling is a simultaneous movement of Rook and King, but most chessplayers refrain from demonstrations of ambidexterity.)

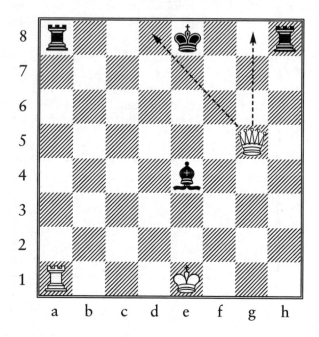

These rules for castling may seem strange, but they are a consequence of the special importance of the King in the game of chess. The unique position of the King, that he must at all costs be preserved and protected from attacks, is one of the main features which distinguish chess from other board games in which the object may be simply to eliminate all the opponent's men. In chess, the ultimate objective is solely to capture the enemy King. Capture of his other pieces may only be a means to facilitate the final chase and submission of His Majesty.

Check and checkmate

When the King is threatened with capture by a hostile piece, it is said to be **in check** from that piece. Since the King must be preserved from capture, the rules specify that the player whose King is in check must immediately play a move to nullify the attack on his King. (The announcement of 'check' used to be mandatory under the rules of the game; this is no longer the case.) The diagram position below shows the White King in check from the Black Rook. The arrowed moves indicate White's possible replies and illustrate the three possible ways of responding to a check:

1 The King may move to a square on which he is no longer under attack;

2 The checking piece may be captured;

3 A piece may be interposed between King and checking piece to interrupt the line of action so that the King is no longer in check.

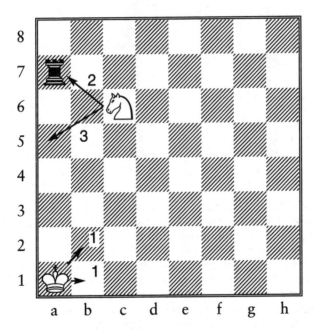

One of these modes of escaping from check must be employed. There is no question of leaving one's King in check in the hope that the opponent will not notice. That is simply against the rules.

Neither is it permissible to counterattack by ignoring one's own King's safety and threatening the opponent's King. The first King to fall loses the game, so retaliatory regicide is not permitted.

If there is no legal move available which allows a checked King to escape – no piece can interpose or capture the checking piece, and the King cannot move anywhere out of attack – then the King is said to be in **checkmate** and the game is over, lost by the side whose King is checkmated. The diagram below gives an example of checkmate. Black's King is in check from the Rook; it cannot advance to escape from the check, because those squares are controlled by the White King or the White Knight.

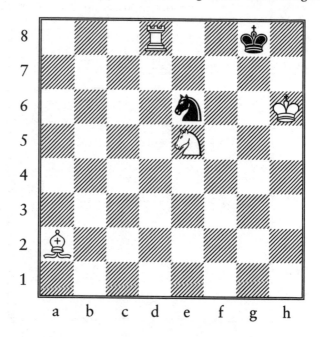

At first sight it may seem that the White Rook can be captured by the Black Knight, but that is impossible since it would leave Black's King in check from the Bishop. So the game is over, and White is the winner. More examples of checkmate will be found in the positions for practice at the end of this chapter.

Stalemate

Finally, what happens if a player is not in check, but he has no legal move which does not leave his King in check? In that case we have reached what is called **stalemate** and the game is a draw. In normal parlance, stalemate is used to signify almost any state of dynamic equilibrium, particularly in political or military situations where each side in a conflict cannot make progress for fear of a devastating response from the other. In chess, however, stalemate has only this single technical usage: a position in which the side to move is not in check, but has no legal move available. Under the laws of the game, the result is then declared a draw. The diagram below illustrates a possible stalemate. Black to play is not in check, but none of his pieces can make a legal move without exposing the King to check.

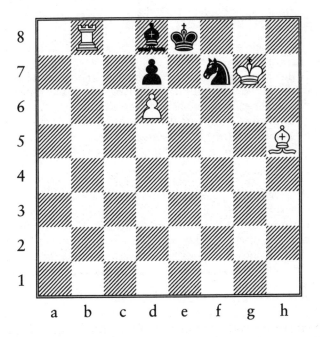

Though only a comparatively rare occurrence, stalemate has an important role to play in the defence of some difficult endgame positions where only a few pieces remain on the board. Many are the unfortunate beginners, too, who have blundered into stalemating their opponent's lone Kings when expectantly closing in for the kill with vast superiority in forces.

So far, we have seen two ways of ending the game: checkmate and stalemate. In practice, a game of chess does not usually go this far. Especially at a high level of play, when one side realizes that he is hopelessly behind, and knows that his opponent has the skills to pursue his advantage to victory, he does not carry on the struggle to the bitter end, with his King checkmated. Rather offer a timely resignation and begin another game in the hope of better fortune.

Just as a game may be won by checkmate or the opponent's resignation, there is more than one way for a game to be drawn. We have already met the draw by stalemate. Our final addition to the rules of chess is to explain other manners of draw.

Draws other than stalemate

1 **Draw by agreement** Just as a player may resign when he realizes his cause is hopeless, the two players may agree to call the game a draw if they agree that neither is getting anywhere and to continue would be pointlessly boring. In such circumstances, one player may 'offer a draw', which his opponent may accept or decline. In the case of acceptance, the game is over and the honour shared; in the case of a draw offer being declined, play simply proceeds as though nothing has happened.

2 **Draw by repetition** This is the rule which permits termination of a game if the pieces are just moving backwards and forwards. Specifically, if the same position has occurred three times on the board, with the same player to move in each case, then a draw may be claimed. In practice this almost always occurs when both sides are moving a single piece each, backwards and forwards, but the rule does apply also to circuitous routes of reaching identical positions. All that matters is that the positions of all the pieces on the board are identical at three distinct moments in the game, and that it is the same player's turn to move on each occasion. (In fact the rule was recently further refined to specify also that the same possibilities, such as castling and en passant, are available in the position on each occasion, but such subtleties need not concern us at this stage.)

3 **The Fifty-move Rule** This is another device to prevent the game meandering on pointlessly. If 50 moves have been made by each side, without either moving a Pawn or making a capture, then the game may be declared drawn if either side wishes.

Neither of these last two rules need really concern the beginner, but we mention them here for the sake of completeness.

Those then are the basic rules of chess. Each piece with its own distinct move, cooperating with the others to try to checkmate the enemy King. How to set about that task will be the theme of the remainder of this book. Our last duty now is to become familiar with chess notation.

Notation

Unfortunately there are two different modes of chess notation currently prevalent in English-speaking countries. The old 'Descriptive Notation' is gradually fading away (but not without a fight) before giving way to the simpler 'Algebraic Notation'. The latter will be used throughout this book. Since a few newspaper columns and most old chess books are written in the other notation, we all eventually have to become bilingual. For this reason, an outline of the Descriptive system is provided at the end of this book, in the Appendix. Let us now proceed with the Algebraic system of chess notation.

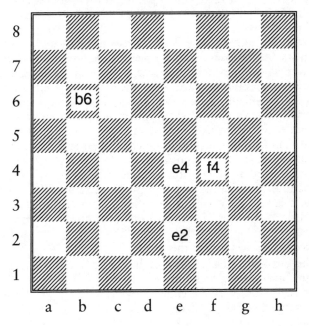

Firstly, the squares of the chessboard: as mentioned earlier, the files are lettered a–h from left to right as White views the board. The ranks are numbered 1–8 from near to far from White's side. Each square thus acquires a unique coordinate corresponding to its file and rank. The sixth square on the b-file is known as b6. The fourth square on the f-file is f4 and so on. If White moves the Pawn in front of his King two squares forward at the start of a game, that Pawn advances from e2 to e4. The pieces themselves are identified by their initial letters: K (King), Q (Queen), B (Bishop), R (Rook) and (with a little poetic licence, to avoid confusion with King) N for Knight. The humble Pawn is left without any identifying symbol.

In order to record any move on the chessboard, it is usually sufficient to write the symbol of the piece moved, together with the coordinates of the square to which it moves. Thus Nf3 means that a Knight has moved to square 3 on the f-file. Ra5 signifies a Rook move to the fifth square on the a-file. Remember that the numbering is always from *White's* side of the board. The Black King and Queen always begin the game on e8 and d8 respectively. In the case of a Pawn move, we just write the square to which the Pawn moves, the absence of any piece symbol being taken as a sign that a Pawn has moved. Moves are numbered (either from the very start of a game or from the start of play from an indicated position), a single number including the White move and Black reply. A few moves will indicate how the system works. From the initial position, play may begin:

1 e3 Nc6   *2* c4 a5   *3* Nc3 Nb4

You should have reached the following position:

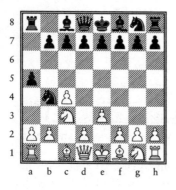

Now suppose White wishes to move his Knight from g1 to e2. It is not sufficient to write Ne2, because either White Knight can be moved to that square. In this case we specify Nge2 (meaning the Knight on the g-file goes to e2) or we could write N1e2 (the Knight on the first rank moves to e2). In either case the additional symbol, between the piece-letter and the square-coordinates, distinguishes between two similar pieces which can play to the same square.

So let us continue this imaginary game:

4 Nge2 Nd3, reaching the diagram position shown below

and it is all over. The White King is in check from the Knight. The King cannot move (you cannot capture your own pieces) and the checking piece cannot be taken. There is no question of interposing any piece along the checking line, because the Knight's mode of travel does not allow any such interruption. White is checkmated and the game is over.

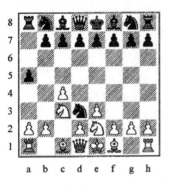

That interlude was our first complete game, but it interrupted the explanation of chess notation. Just two further points: captures are signified by the symbol 'x' between piece and square. So Nxb5 means that a Knight makes a capture on square b5. The captured piece is not identified. In the case of a Pawn capture, we identify the capturing Pawn by the letter corresponding to its file. So bxc5 means that a Pawn from the b-file has made a capture on square c5. Finally, the symbol '+' is used to signify a move which delivers check. For checkmate, we write simply 'mate'.

For ease of reference, there follows a summary of the rules of chess and the manner of notation which will be followed throughout this book.

Summary

Moves of the pieces

Rook – straight lines, up, down or sideways.

Bishop – straight lines, diagonally on the same-colour squares.

Queen – like a Rook or Bishop, straight or diagonal.

King – one square in any direction, but never to any square under attack by an enemy piece.

Pawn – Always forward, one or two squares at first, then one square at a time; may promote to Q, R, N or B on reaching far edge of board. Captures diagonally.

Capturing – by taking the place of the captured piece (except in case of special en passant rule for Pawn captures).

Check – When the King is attacked by an enemy piece; must be countered by moving King, or capturing checking piece, or interposing along checking line.

Checkmate – Check which cannot be countered; end of game.

Stalemate – No legal move not leaving King in check, but King not in check at the time. Draw.

Other draws – By agreement, threefold repetition of position, or fifty moves without Pawn move or capture.

Notation

From White's side – files a–h, ranks 1–8, giving each square a unique pair of coordinates from a1 to h8.

Pieces identified as K, Q, R, N, B (nothing for Pawn).

Kd6 means King moves to square d6, etc.

Kxd6 – King captures on square d6.

Nxd5+ – Knight captures on d5, giving check.

Nexd5+ – Knight from e-file captures on d5 with check.

0-0 and 0-0-0 signifies King's side and Queen's side castling, respectively.

Exercises (answers on page 21)

1 The Knight's move sometimes presents a problem in familiarization; the following problems may be used to provide practice.

   (a) What is the shortest number of moves needed for a Knight to travel from one square to an adjacent square of opposite colour?

   (b) How many moves to reach a diagonally adjacent square?

   (c) How many moves to reach h8 starting at a1?

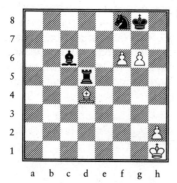

2 Which side can give immediate checkmate, if it is his turn to move in this position?

3 Black to play here checks the White King with 1 . . . b5+ (the three dots before the move indicate that it is a Black move). Is this checkmate? What happens now?

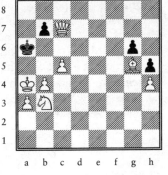

Answers

1a A Knight takes three moves to make such a one-square trip. For example, to reach b1 from a1, it may move a1-b3-d2-b1, or a1-c2-a3-b1.

1b Only two moves, in general; for example, from c3 to d4, it may travel via b5 or via e2. The only exception is when one of the two squares is a corner square. The trip from a1 to b2 takes four moves (the Knight does not have the turning space to do it in two moves).

1c Six moves; for example a1-b3-d4-e6-f4-g6-h8. Note that the Knight changes the colour of the square it occupies each move, so a trip between two black squares must take an even number of moves.

2 Either side could deliver checkmate. If it is White's move, then 1 f7 is mate. The Pawn threatens the King, which cannot move to any square not under fire from the White Bishop or Pawn. Neither can the Pawn be captured by Black's King, since it is defended by the other White Pawn.

If it is Black's move, any move by the Rook will put the White King in check from the Bishop (such a check by a non-moving piece is termed a 'discovered check'). The one such move which denies the White King any escape square is *1* ... Rg5, preventing 2 Kg1 because of the check from the Rook.

3 After *1* ... b5+, White's King has no move to escape from the check, but it is not checkmate. The only move is to capture the Pawn en passant. So White plays *2* c**x**b6 e.p. (en passant captures are generally recorded in this manner – the White c-Pawn makes a capture on b6, note, not on b5). If we look at the resulting position, we see that Black is in stalemate. None of his men can move without exposing his King to check, but he is not in check at the moment. The game is a draw.

elementary endgames

In this chapter you will learn:
- how to drive a lone king to the end of the board and checkmate him
- the basic mates with K+Q, or K+R, and the more complex procedures with K+2B, or K+B+N
- everything you need to know about the subtlety of K+P against K
- how to finish your opponent off at the end of a game, and you will be beginning to understand how simple plans can be formulated and carried out.

At first sight, it may seem paradoxical that we start our discussion of chess with the endgame, but there is no better way to familiarize oneself with the powers of the pieces than to study positions where only few men remain on the board. Their paths are unhampered by other pieces and the uncluttered board allows them full scope. In this chapter, we shall look at the procedures needed to win the game, if indeed it can be won, when the opponent has been reduced to a lone King. For the sake of consistency in the examples, we shall always give the White side the benefit of the extra forces, pursuing a lone Black King.

As will be seen, the principle is almost always the same: restrict the enemy King to a portion of the board by erecting a barrier with one's own men through which he cannot pass. The King's range is then gradually decreased until he is forced to the edge, or in some cases to the very corner, of the board, where he is finally checkmated.

As we shall see, King and Rook or King and Queen are sufficient to force checkmate against King, but King and Bishop or King and Knight cannot win. King and two Bishops or King, Bishop and Knight can win, but King and two Knights ought not to (though there are positions where checkmate is possible, given some cooperation from the opponent). The final section of this chapter will be devoted to positions with King and Pawn against King. In such cases it is a question of whether the Pawn can be forced through to the end of the board to become a Queen. As we shall see, the play in such an endgame can be very delicate and subtle.

Checkmate with two Rooks

This endgame gives a simple and dynamic demonstration of the power of Rooks and also the clearest display of a forcing back procedure. The White King plays no part. From the diagram position overleaf, play continues **1 Rh4 Kf5 2 Ra5+** (one Rook controls the fourth rank, preventing the Black King from advancing, the other gives check, to force him further back) **2 ... Kg6 3 Rb4 Kf6 4 Rb6+ Ke7 5 Ra7+ Kd8 6 Rb8 mate.**

The procedure was sufficiently simple to repeat the same trick, each time one rank further down the board. The side with the two Rooks may, of course, choose instead to force the King to its doom on the first rank instead of the eighth, or to meet its end on the a- or h-file. One edge of the board is much the same as any other once the Pawns have disappeared from the scene of battle.

Now we shall see that in fact one of those Rooks was strictly superfluous to requirements, since King and Rook alone is sufficient to win, but here the White King plays an essential part in the procedure.

Checkmate with one Rook

Begin in the position of the previous diagram, but with the Rook on a2 removed from the board. Play may continue *1* **Kb2 Kd5** *2* **Kc3 Ke5** *3* **Kd3 Kd5** *4* **Rh5+**.

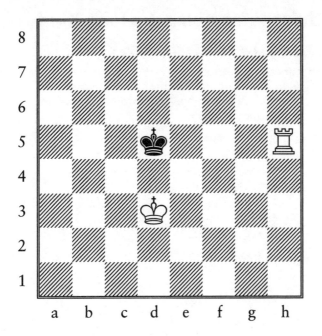

This is the standard formation designed to force the Black King to give ground. The Rook checks while the White King stands guard to prevent the advance of Black's monarch.

To continue: *4 . . . Kd6   5 Ke4 Kc6   6 Kd4 Kb6   7 Kc4 Kc6   8 Rh6+* (reaching the same formation, one rank further down the board) *8 . . . Kd7   9 Kd5 Ke7   10 Ra6* (waiting) *Kf7   11 Ke5 Kg7   12 Kf5 Kf7* (or *12 . . . Kh7   13* Rg6 Kh8   *14* Kf6 Kh7   *15* Kf7 Kh8   *16* Rh6 mate) *13 Ra7+ Ke8   14 Ke6 Kd8   15 Rh7* (waiting) *Kc8   16 Kd6 Kb8 17 Kc6 Ka8   18 Kb6 Kb8   19 Rh8 mate*.

Note, incidentally, that *19* Rb7 on the final move would be an example of stalemate. In chess notation the signs ! and ? are used to indicate good and bad moves, respectively. We would certainly adorn *19* Rb7 with ?? – a very bad move indeed.

King and Rook can in fact force mate against King in at most thirteen moves from any position. The optimal strategy involves a readiness to switch one's objective from a mate on the back rank, as illustrated above, to a mate on the a- or h-file according to the direction the enemy King runs.

Other mates against a lone King

King and Queen against King

Strictly speaking this section ought to be unnecessary, since King and Queen can mate in exactly the same manner as King and Rook. The Queen's extra powers, however, do add some further points worth mentioning.

In the diagram position, White has two moves which give immediate checkmate: *1 Qd8* or *1 Qb7*.

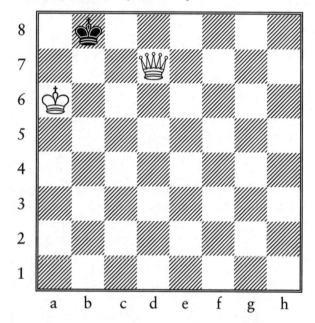

Neither of these moves would be checkmate with a Rook. Note also that *1 Qc6??* would deliver stalemate and a draw. Another stalemate position would be with the Black King on a8, White Queen on b6 or c7 and White's King anywhere at all. The Queen is just powerful enough to stalemate on her own, but she needs the aid of the King to deliver checkmate.

The mating positions with Rook or Queen against King should be understood and remembered. They translate with surprising ease into apparently complex middlegame positions.

King and Two Bishops against King

One may easily convince oneself that there is no mating position with King and Bishop against King (although stalemate is possible). King and two Bishops, however, can force victory, provided, of course, the Bishops operate on opposite coloured squares. Remember, it is possible to have two white-squared Bishops or two black-squared Bishops following a Pawn promotion. Let us begin then with White's King and both Bishops on their home squares, e1, c1 and f1, and the Black King on e8. After the moves **1 Ke2 Ke7 2 Ke3 Ke6 3 Ke4 Kd6 4 Be3 Kc6 5 Bc4 Kd6 6 Bd4** we reach the diagram position.

Note how the Bishops on adjacent squares effectively control interlocking diagonals to restrict the Black King to a triangle of twelve squares from a8 to c6 and d6 to f8. The mating process consists in shrinking this triangle:

6 ... Kc6 7 Ke5 Kd7 8 Bd5 Kc7 9 Bc5 Kd7 10 Bd6 Kd8 11 Be6 Ke8. Now the King is confined to the back rank; the final stage is to force him into a corner where checkmate will be delivered:

12 Kf6 Kd8   13 Bb8 (waiting) **Ke8   14 Bc7 Kf8   15 Bd7 Kg8   16 Kg6 Kf8   17 Bd6+ Kg8   18 Be6+ Kh8   19 Be5 mate.** The final zig-zag process is particularly attractive.

King, Bishop and Knight against King

By far the most difficult of the 'elementary' mates, the Bishop and Knight mate necessitates forcing the enemy King not only to the edge, but right to the corner of the board. A forced mate is in fact only possible in the corner of the same colour as that of the squares upon which the Bishop travels. (Mate in the other corners is possible, but only if the defence errs.)

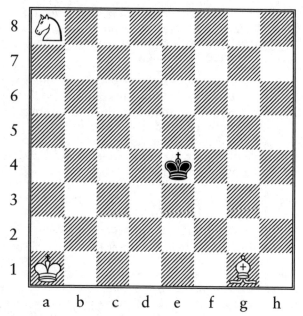

Begin in the diagram position, which is just about as bad as White could imagine in this endgame. The first stage must be to bring the white pieces closer together: **1 Kb2 Kd3   2 Nc7 Kc4 3 Ne6 Kd5   4 Nd4 Kc4   5 Kc2 Kd5   6 Kd3 Kc5   7 Bh2 Kd5   8 Nb3.** We have now reached a typical position in which Black must retreat. Note how White King, Bishop and Knight cooperate to control squares round the Black King. **8 ... Kc6 9 Kc4 Kb6   10 Nc5 Kc6   11 Na4! Kb7   12 Kb5 Kc8   13 Kc6 Kd8   14 Kd6 Kc8** (or **14 . . . Ke8   15 Ke6 Kf8   16 Be5!** and the Black King does not escape) **15 Nb6+ Kb7   16**

Kc5 Ka6   17 Kc6 Ka5   18 Bd6 Ka6. Finally the King must be driven away from a8 towards a1 where the Bishop will deliver mate. *19 Bb8!* Ka5   *20 Nd5!* Ka4 (making a run for it; instead *20 . . .* Ka6 demands less accuracy from White after *21* Nb4+ Ka5   *22* Kc5 Ka4   *23* Kc4 Ka5   *24* Bc7+ continuing the inexorable process towards a1) *21* Kc5 Kb3   *22* Nb4! Kc3   *23* Bf4! Kb3   *24* Be5 Ka4   *25* Kc4 Ka5   *26* Bc7+ Ka4   *27* Nd3 Ka3   *28* Bb6 (waiting) Ka4   *29* Nb2+ Ka3 *30* Kc3 Ka2   *31* Kc2 Ka3   *32* Bc5+ Ka2   *33* Nd3 Ka1 *34* Bd6 Ka2   *35* Nc1+ Ka1   *36* Be5 mate.

The most difficult part of the whole procedure is the manoeuvre between moves 20 and 24, where Black's King appears to be set free, only to find himself once again imprisoned by White's pieces. The whole technique is an instructive example of using one's pieces cooperatively, while it also illustrates well what a cumbersome piece the Knight can be when it is trying to change its object of attack at close range.

In all these examples of checkmates against a lone King, the attacker occasionally made use of a waiting move. In chess, the compulsion to move can sometimes be a disadvantage. When there are many pieces on the board, a move can usually be found which improves one's position, but in the endgame often only a retreat is available when one would prefer to stand one's ground. Indeed, if the privilege of 'passing' were allowed, none of the mates with Rook, two Bishops, or Bishop and Knight, would be able to be forced at all. This explains partly why so few of White's moves in the Bishop and Knight mate are checking moves. White's pieces are used to control squares round the Black King; there is no need to attack the King directly since he must move anyway. Indeed White cannot spare the resources to control the King's square as well as its important retreats. Beginners are often tempted by the chance of a check, but in such endgames there are usually better tasks for one's pieces. As an exercise, you might like to attempt the King and Rook mate, without giving any check before the final checkmate. As will be seen, the process of gradual restriction is in fact more efficient than the forcing back by checking process given earlier.

Some comments on the endgame of King and two Knights against King will be found at the end of this chapter. Such technical endgames as these are rarely encountered in practical play, but the endgame we now discuss is of vital importance as perhaps the most commonly encountered finish to a closely contested game.

King and Pawn against King

The essential position to understand in this endgame is shown in the diagram below. Whichever side is to move, the game should end in a draw, but Black must play accurately to avoid letting the Pawn through to become a Queen.

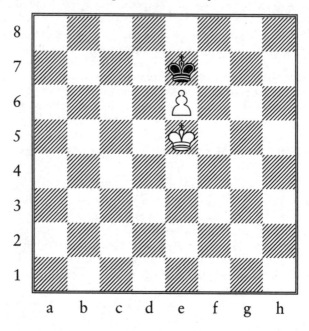

With Black to play the only move is *1 . . . Ke8!* There may follow *2 Kd6 Kd8   3 e7+ Ke8* and now *4 Ke6* is stalemate, while other moves lose the Pawn. Equally, after *1 . . . Ke8!   2 Kf6 Kf8   3 e7+ Ke8   4 Ke6* is again stalemate.

Suppose instead Black had defended inaccurately with *1 . . . Kd8?* Then after *2 Kd6 Ke8   3 e7* we have the same position but with Black, not White to move. He must give ground with *3 . . . Kf7* when *4 Kd7* followed by *5 e8=Q* will win for White. The same happens, of course, after *1 . . . Kf8   2 Kf6 Ke8   3 e7 Kd7   4 Kf7*, etc.

With White to move in the diagram position, he can do nothing to improve matters: *1 Kd5 Ke8!   2 Kd6 Kd8* or *1 Kf5 Ke8! 2 Kf6 Kf8* reach positions we have already examined. The important point is that Black must be able to answer Kd6, whenever it happens with Kd8 and Kf6 must be met by Kf8 to ensure that the critical position, with the Pawn one square from queening, is reached with the right player to move.

From this example, it follows that once the defender has occupied the square in front of the Pawn, he has little to worry about. For example, set up the position: White King on e3, Pawn on e4, Black King on e5. Play may continue *1* Kd3 Ke6 *2* Kd4 Kd6 *3* e5+ Ke6 *4* Ke4 Kd7 (the purist will always play *4* ...Ke7, but even the text move is good enough) *5* Kd5 Ke7 *6* e6 Ke8! and the draw is safe. Black has considerable freedom in his choice of earlier King moves, but when the Pawn reaches the sixth rank, he must take care.

If White's King is in front of his Pawn, however, it may be a totally different story.

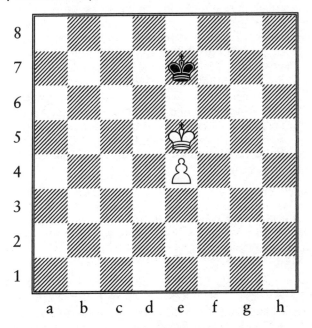

In this position, Black to move loses:

1 ...Kd7 *2* Kf6! Ke8 *3* Ke6 Kf8 *4* Kd7 followed by the Pawn's direct march to the queening square. White's King prepares its path by outflanking the enemy King. Equally after *1* ...Kf7 *2* Kd6 Kf6 (*2* ...Ke8 *3* Ke6 or *2* ...Kf8 *3* Kd7) *3* e5+ Kf7 *4* Kd7 and again the road is prepared for Pawn's advance. If, however, it is White's move in the diagram position, then he can only draw against best play: 1 Kf5 Kf7! or 1 Kd5 Kd7! and Black cannot be outflanked. After 1 Kf5 Kf7! 2 e5 Ke7 3 e6 Ke8! we are back in familiar territory, safe for Black.

Now let us move all the pieces one square up the board; White's King on e6, Pawn on e5; Black King on e8. In this case, White wins whoever has the move. With Black to play: 1 ... Kd8 2 Kf7 or 1 ... Kf8 2 Kd7 ensures the triumph of the Pawn. With White to play, Black is still unable to reach the desired drawn position: 1 Kd6 Kd8 2 e6 Ke8 3 e7 and it is Black's move; he must give ground with 3 ... Kf7 when 4 Kd7 wins as usual.

Finally, let us move the pieces all one square back from their diagram positions: White King on e4, Pawn on e3; Black King on e6. Again with White to move, he can do no better than draw: 1 Kf4 Kf6 or 1 Kd4 Kd6 2 Ke4 Ke6 3 Kf4 Kf6 and Black prevents the White King from gaining ground. But with Black to play, White can win. For example, 1 ... Kd6 2 Kf5! Ke7 3 Ke5! (but not 3 e4 Kf7! 4 Ke5 Ke7! drawing) 3 ... Kf7 4 Kd6 Kf6 5 e4 Kf7 6 e5 Ke8 7 Ke6! Kd8 8 Kf7!, etc. Always the White King prepares the Pawn's path before it advances, making sure that Black cannot reach the safety of the drawn position we have encountered earlier. As long as the White King can stay in front on his Pawn, he has chances for victory.

These conclusions are largely generalizable for any Pawn except for those on the a-file or h-file. We shall come to those in a moment. First, there is one tricky piece of play worth examining in the case of a Pawn one file in from the edge.

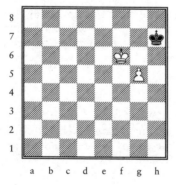

White wins with:

1 Kf7! Kh8 2 Kg6 Kg8 3 Kh6 Kh8 4 g6 Kg8 5 g7 Kf7 6 Kh7, etc.

White must not, however, play 1 g6+?, when 1 ... Kh8! 2 Kf7 gives stalemate or 1 g6+? Kh8! 2 g7+ Kg8 leads to a familiar drawn position.

That example with a g-Pawn showed how the edge of the board can affect the result of a position. The stalemate possibility occurs only because there is no room to the right of the h-file. That has an even greater effect with a Pawn on the very edge file.

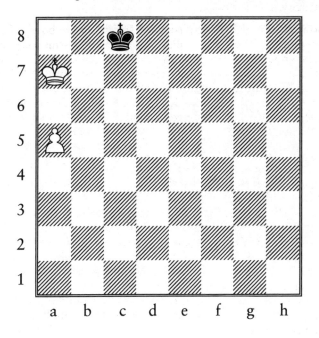

White seems to have all the advantages he could desire in this position, but he can only draw: *1 Kb6 Kb8 2 a6 Ka8 3 a7* stalemates the Black King, while instead *1 a6 Kc7 2 Ka8 Kc8 3 a7 Kc7* leaves White stalemated.

That completes our introduction to the basic checkmates against a lone King and the simple theory of King and Pawn against King. Many more complex positions can reduce to these elementary cases, so it is important to be familiar with them.

Summary

King + Rook, or King + Queen, or King + two Bishops, or King + Bishop + Knight can all force checkmate against a lone King. King + two Knights cannot force mate.

King + Pawn against King is sometimes a win, sometimes a draw. The side with the Pawn should try to prepare its advance by manoeuvring his King in front of the Pawn. The a-Pawn and h-Pawn gives the least chance of victory.

Further examples and exercises

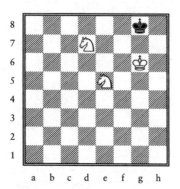

1 If Black plays accurately White can only draw this position. *1 Nf6+ Kh8? 2 Nf7* is mate, but after *1 . . . Kf8!* instead, White can make no progress. Black can only lose such a position by blundering into a one-move mate.

Curiously, if we add a Black Pawn on e6, White can indeed win: *1 Ng4 e5 2 Nh6+ Kh8 3 Nf6 e4 4 Nf7* mate. Without the e-Pawn, Black would be stalemated after White's third move. In fact, there are many positions where two Knights can win against King and Pawn, but the procedure is generally long and complex.

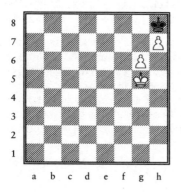

2 This position of King and two Pawns against King looks as though White should win comfortably, but *1 Kh6?* or *1 Kf6* give stalemate. In fact any attempt by the White King to approach closer suffers from the same result. The only way to win involves jettisoning one of the Pawns:

1 Kf5 Kg7 2 h8=Q+! Kxh8 3 Kf6 Kg8 4 g7 Kh7 5 Kf7 and wins.

Both these examples show that the mere existence of a piece on one's own side can actually be a disadvantage. In the second case, White could solve the problem by throwing it overboard.

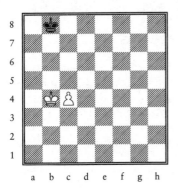

Finally, a more complex example of King and Pawn against King. Black to play in this position; what should the result of the game be?

Try to work it out before reading the explanation below.

The position should be drawn, but only if Black finds the correct first move: *1 ... Kc8!*. The reason for this is as follows: After *1 ... Kc7? 2 Kc5!* or *1 ... Kb7? 2 Kb5!* we reach positions of a type already discussed and winning for White. (For example *1 ... Kc7 2 Kc5 Kb7 3 Kd6 Kc8 4 Kc6 Kb8 5 Kd7* and the Pawn is ready to romp home.) After *1 ... Kc8!* Black keeps open his options and can meet *2 Kc5* with *Kc7!* or *2 Kb5* with *Kb7!* preventing the White King from gaining space in either case. Two Kings with just one empty square between them in such a manner (say on b5 and b7 or c5 and c7) are often said to be *in opposition*. The side who moved last has *taken the opposition* and is ready to follow his opponent (as Black does here to prevent White from gaining space) or to side-step and outflank him (as White does when Black is forced to step aside). The concept of the opposition is a particular example of the more useful one of *related squares*.

In our example above, White's Kb5 must be met by Kb7, and Kc5 must be met by Kc7; thus we have two pairs of related squares (b5, b7) and (c5, c7). On b4 White's King is in touch with both b5 and c5, so Black must stay in touch with b7 and c7. The only possibility therefore is *1 ... Kc8!*. Later in the book we shall see some far more complicated endgames where the concept of related squares provides a simple solution.

03 elementary tactics

In this chapter you will learn:
- the relative values of the different pieces
- how to calculate several moves ahead
- basic tactical themes including the pin, fork, discovered attack, and overloading
- common patterns including smothered mate, back-rank mate, and the draw by perpetual check
- the idea of a combination: where different pieces combine in a sequence of moves to force victory.

The essence of chess thought lies in the ability to calculate correctly future possible continuations of the game, to see what is likely to happen several moves ahead and to select the most promising move on the basis of variations calculated. As we shall see, the task of 'seeing ahead' may be divided into two areas: *tactics* and *strategy*.

Tactics means the precise calculation of forced variations, where one side's moves contain direct threats which must be parried by the other side. Captures of pieces, checking moves, threats of checkmate all come under the heading of tactics. Attacks on larger pieces by smaller ones also demand evasive action and therefore form a part of tactical play.

Strategy is the higher form of chess thought, the long-term planning involved in preparing for later action. Strategic thought is always a far more fuzzy process than the brutal precision of tactics, but in any position the two are inextricably intertwined, with each player's future strategic dreams always having to be viewed in the light of the harsh reality of present tactical opportunities.

Chess players are often asked: 'How many moves do you see ahead?' The question in itself shows a misunderstanding of the thought process of chess. The tactics of a position permit exact calculation, and indeed must be worked out correctly, for the result of the game may be decided by them immediately. In some positions, the tactics are so clear that they may be calculated twenty or more moves ahead with certainty, as in the following example. Both sides are ready to race their Pawns home to queen:

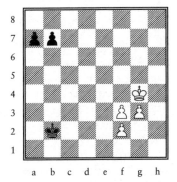

1 f4 a5   2 f5 a4   3 f6 a3
4 f7 a2   5 f8=Q a1=Q. Now White can force an exchange of Queens:

6 Qh8+   Ka2   7 Qxa1+ Kxa1 and the race begins anew:

8 f4 b5   9 f5 b4   10 f6 b3
11 f7 b2   12 f8=Q b1=Q. Once again White can force the continuation:

13 Qa3+   Qa2   14 Qxa2+ Kxa2

15 Kf5 followed by advancing the g-Pawn until it becomes a Queen at move twenty. That twenty-move variation is not hard to visualize from the starting position. On the other hand, there are many positions which allow scarcely any direct calculation of probable continuations. In such cases, considerations will be based on strategic plans and may only grope three or four moves into the future, with no certainty even then. In this chapter we shall be considering the elements which make up tactical play, the hand-to-hand fighting of the chess armies.

Relative values of the pieces

Rooks, Knights, Bishops, Queens and Pawns all have different ways of moving. A Queen can do all that a Rook can, and more. A Rook aided by its King can checkmate the enemy King on an empty board, whereas Bishop or Knight cannot. No surprise then to learn that a Queen is considered superior to a Rook, which in turn is generally worth more than Bishop or Knight. One cannot assign absolute values to the pieces, since circumstances may drastically alter the effectiveness of each piece. As a rough and ready rule, the following scale of values gives an idea of the relative worth of each of the pieces:

Pawn – 1; Bishop – 3; Knight – 3; Rook – 5; Queen – 9.

One cannot assign a value to the King, since his special role in the game puts him beyond such material consideration. In terms of fighting ability, however, a King used as an attacking piece is approximately as effective as a Knight or Bishop. The need to keep him safe from attack, however, prevents the aggressive use of the King until all danger has vanished from the board. If we look at the nature of the other pieces, we can understand better how the above scale of piece values ought to be interpreted.

The Pawn

The humble foot-soldier of chess, weakest of all pieces, but in that very weakness lies the greatest strength of the Pawn. Any other piece must run from the Pawn's attack. If, for example, a Knight or Rook attacks a Pawn, it is sufficient to defend that Pawn with another man. Capturing the Pawn will then entail a net loss. On the other hand, if a Pawn attacks a Knight or Rook, the attacked piece can hardly stand its ground, even if defended by another piece, since its capture will entail loss of Knight or Rook for a mere Pawn.

The Pawns are thus the most effective pieces for controlling terrain on the chess battlefield. Knights, Bishops, Rooks and Queens dare not tread on those squares attacked by Pawns.

As we shall see when we come to discuss strategic planning, the Pawns define the boundaries of each side's territory. A planned and gradual advance of Pawns can gain manoeuvring space for the other pieces and cramp the opponent's men.

Bishops and Knights

Each worth about three Pawns, the Bishop and Knight are so different from one another that it is hard to understand how they can have so close a value. The Bishop is a long-range piece, quick to move from one area of the board to another, but limited always to squares of one colour. Thirty-two of the board's squares are permanently beyond its horizons. The Knight, on the other hand, can get anywhere, given the time.

Generally speaking, if the board is open and uncluttered by numerous Pawns, the Bishop is superior, particularly when there is action at widely separated points. The Bishop in such cases can affect both sides of the board at the same time; it can help with attack, while simultaneously looking backwards towards defence. When the Pawns have become blocked against one another, the diagonals are closed, and play is slow and localized, then the Knight is at its most effective.

While Knight and Bishop are of approximately equal value, the pair of Bishops are more often than not superior to two Knights. We have already seen that two Bishops can checkmate a lone King where two Knights cannot. The two Bishops, operating on different colour squares, complement each other perfectly. They can never impede each other's movements, and between them they can cover the whole board.

The Rook

In the early stages of the game, the Rook has a lesser part to play than its value might suggest. The Rook needs open lines: until some Pawns have been exchanged, the Rooks simply do not have the space they need to operate effectively. Also, since Rooks are fundamentally more valuable than Knights or Bishops, a Rook must run from attack by those lesser pieces. Any Rook brought out onto the open board too early is liable to find itself hounded about by attacks from sniping Bishops and Knights.

The table of values suggests that a Rook and one Pawn is worth about the same as Bishop and Knight, but such an exchange should be viewed with circumspection. Both Rooks and Pawns need time to make their value felt. As a Pawn advances, its eventual threat of becoming a Queen grows more real. As lines become open, the Rooks swing into action. But in the early stages of the game, Bishop and Knight in combination are likely to be more than a match for Rook and Pawn. Despite that, the calculation making Rook equal to Bishop and two Pawns, or Knight and two Pawns, is a fair approximation to the way things work in practice.

The Queen

Worth a little less than two Rooks, about the same as three lesser pieces (or minor pieces as Bishop and Knight are usually known). Interestingly, although the Queen moves like Rook or Bishop, she is worth more than the combined value of those two pieces. This reflects her ability to operate as a Bishop on white or black squares (though not, of course, simultaneously).

Forcing gain of material

The simplest way to gain material on the chessboard is to capture an undefended piece. When beginners start to play, and are still getting used to the moves of the pieces, most games are decided simply by overlooking that pieces are attacked, or by carelessly putting them on squares where they can be taken. Once one has overcome that phase of unfamiliarity with the pieces, such crude mistakes become rare. (I would like to say that they disappear, but sad experience tells that it is not so.) The next stage in the familiarization process is to understand the range of simple tactical tricks which can lead to gain of material in somewhat more sophisticated fashion. What follows in this chapter is a small-arms catalogue for the chessboard warrior.

There are really only two distinct ways of forcing gain of material: attacking two pieces at the same time, or attacking one piece which, for one reason or another, cannot move away. Each of these objectives may be achieved in a number of different ways, the most common of which will be illustrated overleaf. All the ideas involved will be seen to be strongly dependent upon the geometry of the chessboard and the lines of action of the pieces.

In each of the examples which follows, the reader should try to improve his skills at visualizing the result of a series of moves. Set up the position on a board and play through the moves if necessary, but always return to the original position and attempt to re-play the moves in your head, until you are capable of a clear visualization of the variation under consideration and the final position arrived at. This ability is bound to come gradually, and it is an essential part of chess fluency.

The first example of calculation, below, involves working out the result of a series of exchanges of pieces. Here it will be necessary to remember as the variation proceeds that pieces are disappearing from the board. There is no easy way to learn to keep track of such calculations, except by continual practice and increasing experience of the chessboard and pieces.

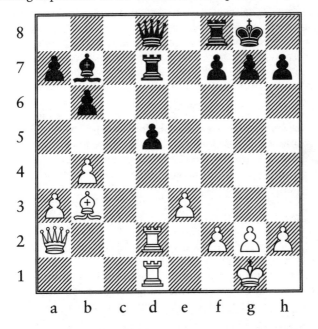

White to play calculates that he can safely capture the d-Pawn. Although only two of his pieces directly attack the Pawn, two more lurk with hidden attacks. Thus *1 Bxd5 Bxd5   2 Rxd5 Rxd5   3 Qxd5 Qxd5   4 Rxd5* and White has emerged with an extra Pawn. White's Queen and Bishop on the diagonal form in effect two attacks on the Pawn, as do his two Rooks on the file. Equally, Black's Queen provides a reserve defence.

Reasoning that White has four effective attackers, while Black has only three defenders, is a tempting but fallacious argument that the Pawn can be taken. The order of capturing is of great importance as we can see if we place the White Queen on d3 instead of a2. White still has four attacks on the Pawn, but *1 Bxd5? Bxd5 2 Qxd5 Rxd5 3 Rxd5* does not compel Black to continue the capturing sequence; after *3 . . . Qf6* White has just lost his Queen for Rook and Pawn. Of course a simple count of attackers and defenders can give a good guide to whether a particular capture is feasible or not, but there is no substitute for a precise calculation of all the moves involved.

The fork

The simplest tactical weapon to ensure gain of material is the **fork**: an attack on two different pieces by the same man. If the attacked pieces are both of higher value than the attacker, or if there is no satisfactory way to leave both pieces defended, then material loss may be inevitable. One of the shortest of all international chess games ended with a drastic fork: after the moves *1 e4 c5 2 d4 cxd4 3 Nf3 e5 4 Nxe5?* Black played *4 . . . Qa5+* when any move meeting the check will be met by *5 . . . Qxe5* leaving Black a Knight ahead. The fork of King and Knight after Black's fourth move gives White no time to attend to both the attacks in a single move.

Unguarded pieces in the centre of the board are particularly susceptible to fall victim to a fork by the enemy Queen. Keeping all one's pieces protected all the time, even if it were possible, would be far too defensive an attitude, but special vigilance should be given to those of one's men which are not defended and are liable to attack by enemy pieces.

Since any piece may attack an enemy piece, it follows that any piece – even a King – may deliver a fork by attacking two enemy pieces simultaneously. The most commonly encountered, however, and the most easily overlooked is the Knight fork.

Here White can fork King and Rook with Nc7+ or King and Queen with Nf6+. In either case the King must move, leaving the other piece to be captured.

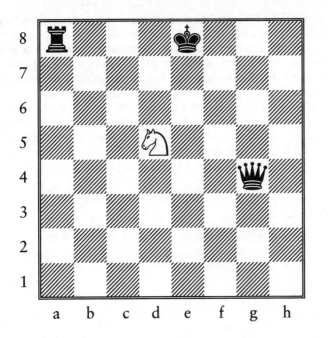

Many are the Rooks in the corner which have been lost, before they have even made a single move, to such a fork by a Knight.

The discovered attack

When a piece moves from one square to another, it will generally result in a change in the immediate effect of that piece. New squares will be attacked and defended, new threats created. After each move, one must naturally look at those changes to see what immediate action must be taken. But also the mere act of vacating a square can have important consequences. Lines of action previously blocked can suddenly become open for other pieces. When one piece steps aside to reveal an attack by another, we speak of a **discovered attack**.

In the position shown, White, for all his material inferiority, can use the theme of discovered attack to win the game. After *1 Rxg7+ Kh8* the scene is set for a Rook move to discover a check from the Bishop: *2 Rxf7+ Kg8 3 Rg7+ Kh8 4 Rxd7+ Kg8*. By now the theme should be clear. White has a simply operating mechanism, allowing Black no option each time but to submit to the mercies of Rook and Bishop. *5 Rg7+ Kh8 6 Rxc7+ Kg8 7 Rg7+ Kh8 8 Rxb7+ Kg8 9 Rg7+ Kh8 10 Rxa7+ Kg8 11 Rg7+ Kh8 12 Rc7+ Kg8 13 Rxc8* and White is set for victory.

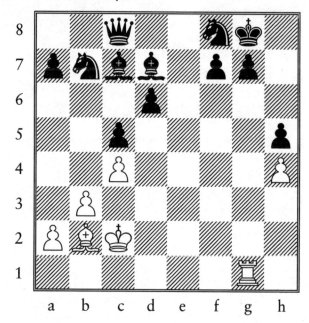

The discovered check is almost equivalent to a free move with the discovering piece. While the opponent is escaping from the check, that piece can do its worst. Of course, if the opponent's King is not at the end of the discovery, the effect is considerably lessened, but it can be as devastating for a vital attack to be discovered by a piece itself giving check.

In the diagram opposite, Black to play is set to discover an attack on the White Queen by moving his Knight. Playing *1 ... Nb4+* (or *1 ... Nd4+*) he ensures that the next move he will be

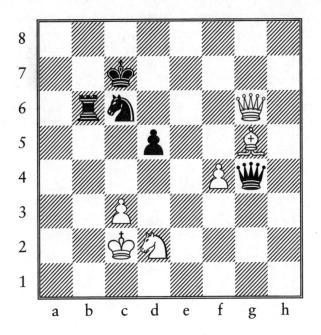

able to play is *2 ... Rxg6*. Even if the Knight is captured, Black will gain Queen or Knight from the venture. Equally, if White is to play in the same position, he will move *1 Bd8+* followed by *2 Qxg4* gaining Queen for Bishop.

As with the fork, the theme of the discovered attack is that of attacking two enemy pieces at the same time. The lesson here is to look beyond one's own men which appear to be blocking their colleagues. The blockage may be purely temporary. The Black Knight on c6 only lessens rather than cancels the effort of the Rook along the rank from d6 to h6; and the presence of the White Bishop on g5 does not guarantee a safe life for the Black Queen on g4.

The pin

Even simpler than attacking two pieces at the same time is to attack one piece which cannot, or dare not, move away. The **pin** is one of the simplest ways to immobilize an enemy piece.

In this diagram position, White can immobilize the Black Knight by playing *1 Ba4*. The Knight cannot move away without leaving the Black King in check from the Bishop. The Bishop is said to *pin* the Knight to the King. After *1 . . . Kd7*, Black defends his Knight, but the pin is not broken. Advancing his Pawn with *2 d5*, White ensures that he will win the Knight. It cannot move away and will be captured next move by Pawn or Bishop.

When a piece is pinned in such a manner to the King, the pin is absolute. The pinned piece cannot legally move away. But it can be almost equally immobilizing to have a piece pinned to the Queen or Rook. If we replace the Black King by a Queen in the position above, after *1 Ba4* the Knight is again pinned and cannot move without exposing the Queen to possible capture by the Bishop. In this case, however, there is a remedy in the shape of discovered attack: *1 . . . Nxd4+!* followed by *2 . . . Qxa4*, a tactical resource allowed by the position of the White King.

The essential feature of a pin is a piece immobilized by its duty of shielding a more important piece from attack. The following diagram illustrates a closely related tactic with the roles of the attacked pieces transposed.

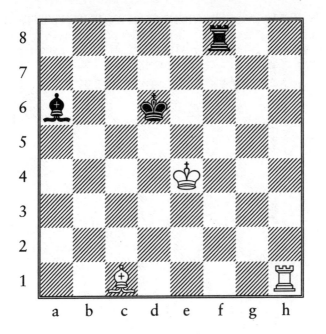

White to play can win a Rook by *1 Ba3+*. Black's King must move out of attack, revealing an attack by the Bishop on the Rook. Equally, White could begin *1 Rh6+* and capture the Bishop on a6 after the King moves away.

If Black is to move in the diagram position he plays *1 ... Bb7+* to win the Rook on h1. Such attacks on one piece through another are sometimes called *X-ray attacks* or *skewers*. They combine geometrical features of both the pin and the discovered attack.

As one becomes familiar with these different types of tactic, one begins to develop an awareness for the presence of pieces on the same diagonal, rank or file. When, for example, Queen and King stand on the same file, it is natural to look for an enemy Rook which can move to that file to win the Queen by pin or X-ray. If King and Queen are on the same diagonal, one must be alert for a possible Bishop move onto that diagonal.

Simple tactics such as those described above are no more than one-move tricks to gain material advantage. In general, the complete tactical resources of a position will involve a complex interaction of these and other elementary units. When more than one piece, or more than one tactical idea, is involved in a forcing sequence of moves in a chess game, we have what is known as a **combination**. The diagram below gives a neat but simple example of a combination.

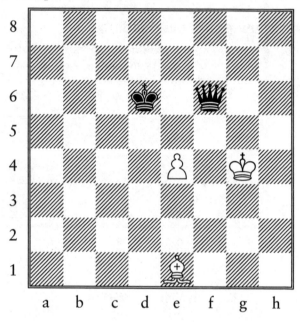

White begins with *1* e5+ (Pawn fork). If the Pawn is not captured, Black will lose his Queen. But *1* . . . Kxe5 is met by *2* Bc3+ (X-ray attack on the Queen), or *1* . . . Qxe5 by *2* Bg3 (pinning the Queen). On White's third move, come what may, he will be able to capture the Black Queen. Note how the initial Pawn advance in this short sequence forced the Black King and Queen onto the same diagonal, either a1–h8 or h2–b8, where the Bishop could then perform its duties. As White's most dynamic forcing move, *1* e5+ should be the first possibility one looks at in the position. Continuing with each of Black's available replies, the rest of the combination should be readily discovered. The difficulty of any combination often consists mainly in forcing oneself to give serious consideration to an introductory move (such as *1* e5+ above) which at first sight just leaves a man to be captured. In fact, one should give at least cursory examination to any move which severely restricts the opponent's choice of reply.

That example was only a diversion from the theme of elementary tactical ideas, to show how they can build into more complex structures. We have still to introduce two more of the bricks for such structures.

Undermining and overloading

When a piece has an important defensive duty to perform, that piece can be as tied to its post as if it were pinned. In the diagram position, the Black Knight on c6 guards the a7 Pawn and is the only obstacle to White's playing *1* Qxa7 mate.

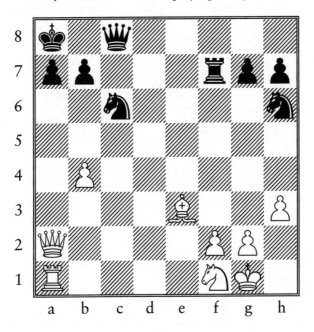

By attacking the Knight with *1* **b5** White sets about undermining the defender of a7. *1* . . . Na5 would be met simply by *2* Qxa5, while other Knight moves all allow Qxa7 mate. So the Knight would have to be given up. An even simpler example of undermining a defender can be seen on the other side of the board. The Knight on h6 defends the Rook on f7. By playing *1* **Bxh6** White gains a Knight since *1* . . . gxh6 allows *2* Qxf7. It is not enough to think complacently that all one's pieces are defended, it is necessary also that those defences cannot be undermined by capture or attack.

The idea behind a successful undermining operation is to eliminate the defender, but it can be equally effective to lure it elsewhere. A piece which tries to combine two important defensive duties can be unreliable when its workload demands that it be in two different places at the same time.

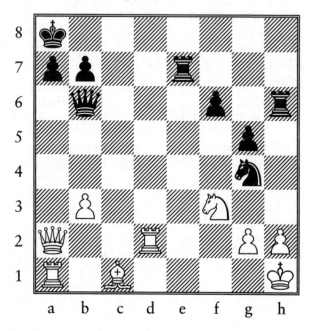

The diagram position gives examples of overloaded pieces. The Black Queen defends against both Rd8 mate and Qxa7 mate. White to move first lures away the defender then kills: *1 Rd8+ Qxd8 2 Qxa7 mate* (or *1* Qxa7+ Qxa7 *2* Rd8 mate). Turning our attention to the other side of the board, it is White's Knight which has too full an in-tray. Called upon to protect both h2 and e1, he cannot cope. Black to play wins with *1 ... Re1+ 2 Nxe1 Rxh2 mate.* (He could also start with *1 ...* Rxh2+ but the mate would take a move longer.)

With the last couple of examples, we complete our introduction to the basic tactical themes, but we have already begun to tread on the ground of the next topic: basic mating patterns. The ultimate object of any chess game is checkmate. Winning the opponent's pieces will be a considerable help in attaining that objective, and we have already seen some of the ways of mating a lone King. But as these last positions have shown, a King can fall victim to checkmate even with many pieces on the board.

You may have noticed certain similarities between the mating positions reached in these examples and those in the previous chapter when the board was down to only a few men. This is no coincidence. There are only a limited number of ways of giving checkmate and the most common of them recur again and again with only minor features altered. As one becomes more familiar with the game, one builds up a repertoire of mating patterns, recognized immediately, just as the learner of a new language expands his vocabulary. Indeed, the psychologist would describe the skill of chess playing as one of pattern recognition. The position on the board is compared in the mind with positions one has previously encountered. Their similarities and differences are noted and old ideas are reassembled to create new combinations and new understanding.

Mating combinations

In the next few pages we shall see how the knowledge of simple mating patterns can help in finding quite complex combinations which may decide the outcome of the game. Much of chess thought might be described as visualizing a desired end position, then working out if such a position can be attained and how. The mating schema which follow give the ideas for the end positions. In the game positions following each mating pattern, the essential details of the pattern are all there, if not quite in the right places to deliver the fatal blow immediately. It is the job of the player to ascertain whether he can force the other bits of the jigsaw into place.

Needless to say, this collection is far from exhaustive. If it were, the game of chess would never have lasted as long as it has. What is important is to see how simple chessboard structures can transplant themselves into apparently more complex positions. Finding the winning continuation in such positions as these is a two-stage process: firstly, the inspirational stage of detecting the relevant idea; and secondly the analytical process of establishing the sequence of moves which can turn the inspiration into reality on the board. Each part of this process is made easier or more difficult by the clues on the board that provide a guiding light towards solution.

The back-rank mate

The theme of the back-rank mate is simple: a Rook or Queen gives check to a King which cannot escape owing to the presence of his own Pawns. Possible variations to the basic pattern include the substitution of a Black Bishop for the Pawn on h7; or a Knight could replace the f7-Pawn, with White's Rook closer in on e8. Leaving a King hemmed in on the back row in this manner is always a source of potential danger. This type of checkmate is one of the most common sudden finishes to games between inexperienced players. Of course, it is only a variation on the endgame mate with King and Rook against King; then it was the White King which replaced the three Black Pawns by standing guard at g6 to refuse any escape square to the Black monarch.

The simplest way to avoid the danger of a back-rank mate is to ensure that the King has an escape square by playing a Pawn to h6 or g6, but, like all chess moves, such a Pawn advance should only be made if there is real need for it.

In the examples on the facing page, we see one long and dazzling variation on this simple theme and one short but difficult game-ending which manages to rotate the idea through ninety degrees.

(i)

From a game Adams–Torre, New Orleans 1920 (the first-named player always has the white pieces):

1 Qg4!   Qb5
2 Qc4!   Qd7
3 Qc7!   Qb5
4 a4   Qxa4
5 Re4!   Qb5
6 Qxb7! resigned.

Throughout this remarkable sequence of moves, Black's Queen and c8-Rook are tied to the defence of the Rook on e8. Any capture of White's Queen would be met by Rxe8+ followed by back-rank mate. After White's fifth move, the e4-Rook is immune (5 . . . Rxe4   6 Qxc8+ Qe8   7 Qxe8+ Rxe8   8 Rxe8 mate). Finally the Black Queen has nowhere to hide and must be lost. Recognising the hopelessness of playing on without his Queen Black conceded the game. (Recent research has cast doubt upon the authenticity of this game, but it is still a beautiful combination, real or invented.)

The next example features a neat defeat of a World Champion.

(ii)

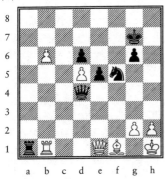

From the game Karpov–Taimanov, Leningrad 1977, the finish with Black to play was:

1 . . . Ng3+! and White resigned.

2 Qxg3 Rxb1 leaves him no real chance, while 2 hxg3 Ra8! leaves no defence against 3 . . . Rh8 mate. Not a back-rank but a side-edge mate.

Smothered mate

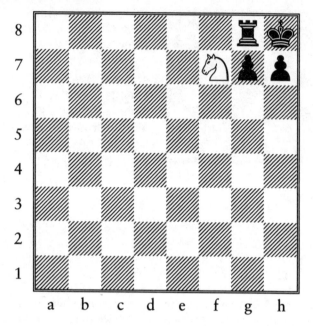

This mate by the Knight is usually known by the picturesque term **smothered mate**. The Black King is smothered to death by his own pieces denying him any escape from a Knight check. As we have seen, one's own pieces getting in the way can often be a cause of problems. Even in the basic Rook mate on the back-rank, there is an element of self-smothering by the Black Pawns.

The shortest possible game ending in checkmate also features a King surrounded by his own pieces. Known as **fool's mate** it is over in two moves: *1 f3 e5 2 g4 Qh4* mate. Note that the Queen does not even avail herself of the ability to move like a Rook, this is a pure Bishop mate.

Smothered mate with a Knight, though a comparatively rare finish to a game, is one of the best chessboard illustrations of the triumph of quality over quantity. Note two important possible variations in the diagram position: the Rook on g8 could equally well be a Knight; or we could give mate with the Knight also on g6, provided we have a White Rook added on h1, pinning the Black h-Pawn to prevent capture of the Knight. The two examples on page 55 both illustrate a common combinational idea which leads to a victory by smothered mate.

(i)

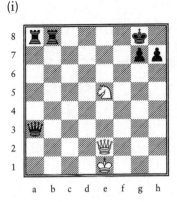

White wins as follows:

1 Qc4+   Kh8
2 Nf7+   Kg8
3 Nh6+   Kh8
4 Qg8+!   Rxg8
5 Nf7   mate.

Note that Black's King cannot flee to f8 on the first or third moves of this sequence, owing to immediate mate by Qf7.

This combination is known as 'Philidor's Legacy' after the great French player (and operatic composer) François Andre Danican Philidor (1726–95). The idea, however, dates back still further to the Spaniard Luis de Lucena in 1497 and subsequently the Italian Gioachino Greco in 1625.

Three hundred years after Greco, the smothered mate was still effective in the game Stolberg–Zak, USSR 1938:

(ii)

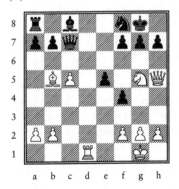

1 Rd7!   Bxd7
2 Qxf7+   Kh8
3 Bc4!   Ng6
4 Qg8+!   Rxg8
5 Nf7   mate.

White's opening move disrupted communications between c7 and f7. His third move threatened Qg8 mate and also set up the mechanism for the smothered mate.

Mating with Queen

The simplest checkmate of all is given by a protected Queen sitting directly in front of a King on the edge of the board.

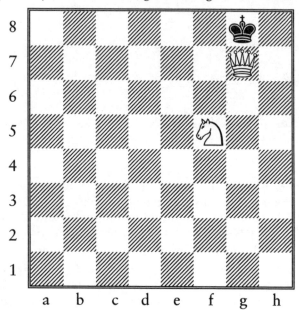

A Queen giving check in such a position will always end the game at once, provided she cannot be captured. A very common variation to this checkmate position is seen by placing the White Queen and Knight one square to the right. With that modification, the King has an escape square on f8, but the position becomes checkmate if f8 is occupied by a Black Rook, Bishop or Queen. The most frequently seen of all short beginners' games ends in just such a mate. Known as **scholar's mate** it runs: *1* e4 e5 *2* Bc4 Bc5 *3* Qh5 Nc6?? *4* Qxf7 mate. On his third move, Black saw the attack on e5 and defended the Pawn with his Knight, overlooking the far more deadly threat to f7. By playing either *3* . . . Qe7 or *3* . . . Qf6 both threats could satisfactorily have been defended and White's Queen later attacked and driven away from her threatening post.

Note that in all these Queen mate positions, it does not matter which piece defends the Queen: Knight, Bishop, Pawn or even King, the Queen herself covers all the possible flight squares of the enemy King, and the only function of the defender is to prohibit Black's capture of Queen with King.

The next position is from a game Betbeder–Tiroler, played in 1930. White's thoughts should be directed by the presence of his Pawn so close to the Black King. If his Queen can join in the attack, the smell of checkmate should be in the air:

(i)

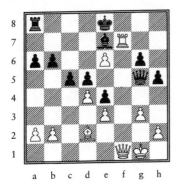

1 Rf8+! Bxf8
2 Qf7+ Kd8
3 Qd7 mate.
The essence of this combination is the Rook's opening clearance of f7 for the Queen. Note that Black's forced capture of the Rook also opens the road for the final Queen move.

The chessplayer's thought process in such a position must, as always, be flexible. It is easy to think: 'I cannot play Rf8+, because he can take it', but forcing oneself to visualize the position after *1 . . . Bxf8*, even momentarily, should reveal the easy mate which follows.

In that example, *1 Rf8+* was a forcing move which gave Black no time to organize his defences. The next position is a famous example of forcing play to reach a desired objective:

(ii)

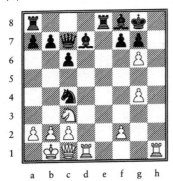

1 Rh8+! Kxh8
2 Rh1+ Kg8
3 Rh8+ Kxh8
4 Qh1+ Qh2
5 Qxh2+ Kg8
6 Qh7 mate.
(Mannheim v Regensberg, played in 1912.)

Mate with Rook and Knight

This mating position with Rook and Knight is a good illustration of the cooperation between two pieces of different types. The Knight both protects the Rook and covers the one possible square on which the Black King would not be in check from the Rook.

There is an interesting variation on this theme if we move the White Rook to d7 and the Black King to g8, in check from the Knight. Then 1 . . . Kh8 will just walk into the above mating position by 2 Rh7, but the alternative King move 1 . . . Kf8 can be met by 2 Nh7+ Ke8 3 Nf6+ Kf8 4 Nh7+ Kg8 5 Nh7+, etc. The Black King can never escape from the Knight checks and White would be able to claim a draw by repetition of position. Such a draw is termed a draw by **perpetual check**, when an endless series of checks forces the harassed King to repeat his moves. Several games have been saved by such a Rook and Knight perpetual check mechanism, with the checking side, of course, well behind on material, but having successfully manoeuvred his Rook and Knight into the right places to force the draw.

The next position is taken from an 1860 game won by the first World Champion, Wilhelm Steinitz. If White's Rook were not in the way Black could mate immediately with *1 . . . Rg1*. This observation should be enough to suggest the winning combination:

(i)

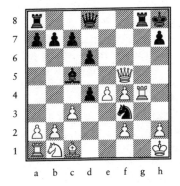

1 . . .   Qh4!
2 Rg2   Qxh2+!
3 Rxh2 Rg1 mate.

Throughout this short sequence, Black is simply taking advantage of the overloaded White Rook, which cannot combine its task of guarding g1 with the job of defending against a Queen and Knight mate.

The next example, from a game Sokolov–Ruzhnikov, USSR 1967, is a more imaginative use of the same idea. Black rejects the chance to promote his Pawn to a Queen, even with check, since White's reply would be to interpose the Rook, discovering check for his own Queen and winning Black's newly crowned lady. Instead his first move is an attempt to chase away the White Queen.

The end is short and drastic:

(ii)

1 . . .   h6
2 Rxb7+! hxg5
3 Nc6+   Ke8
4 Re7   mate.

The usual Rook and Knight mate is translated into the middle of the board, with Black's own Rook plugging the last hole.

The last few pages have given some examples of how ideas on the chessboard can repeat themselves in diverse positions. Each idea is itself the complex expression of a relationship between different pieces on the board. Correctly perceiving those relationships is an essential part of chess understanding and can come only with experience. Each time an essential pattern repeats itself in the experience of an individual player, that pattern is recognized more quickly. In time, each chess position is recognized not as a collection of disparate pieces on the board, but as a coherent series of interrelationships between those pieces. Each move made on the board will change some of those relationships, while leaving others unaltered. The whole position, and the flow of the game, can be seen as a mutating organism, making a sequence of discrete changes of form as each piece is moved.

Most important, therefore, as the game progresses, is to focus attention firstly on the last move played. As soon as the opponent has moved, one should look at that move and ask how it alters one's perception of the game. What new squares are threatened by the moving piece? What lines are possibly opened by the square it vacated? Was the piece performing any important function before it moved, which is now left unattended? And, of course, one should ask exactly the same questions of one's own intended moves before committing them to the board.

Acquiring such a discipline in thought processes is the only way to avoid those grievous mistakes which chessplayers know as blunders. The same discipline helps develop a pattern of thought which can cope with the organization of the widely diverse tactical elements which make up a single position.

Further examples and exercises

1 It is part of essential tactical technique to train oneself to calculate all forcing variations from any position – and there is nothing more forcing than a move that delivers check. Here, for example, White might consider *1* Bf7+ which leads to mate after *2 . . . Rxf7   3 Qxh7*, or *2 . . . Kh8   3 Qxh7*.

Unfortunately, however, Black has a better reply. When you have found it, try looking at other forcing moves for White in the diagram position. One of them forces mate in two moves.

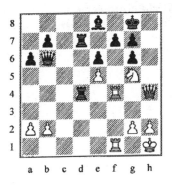

2 Here is a far more complex position: White to move in the game Rosentalis–Nikolic, Moscow 1994. The first thing to look at should be 1 Qh7+ Kf8 2 Qh8+ Ke7 (Black's reply is forced on each occasion). Now 3 Rxf7+ would be mate, if the bishop could not take it, and that should be enough to see 3 Rxf7+ Bxf7 4 Rxf7 mate. The question is, though, what happens after 3 Rxf7+ Kd8? Can you find how White forces mate in a similar, but more brilliant fashion?

Hint: think about the essentials of the mating position after 4 Rxf7 above. The Queen uses only her rook's move to guard the back rank, while a Rook, protected on f7, gives check and the Pawn on e5 prevents an escape to d6. But how does White rid himself of the nuisance of the Bishop on e8?

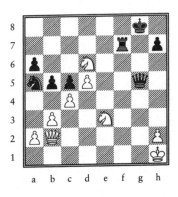

3 Finally, an example of a combination that does not end in checkmate. In this position, from a Petrosian–Spassky world championship match game in 1966, White can play 1 Nxf7, leaving himself a Pawn up after either Kxf7 or Qxe3, but just think how strong Nxf7 would be if it delivered check. The essence of any combination is to force the opponent's pieces into a desired geometrical configuration. What is the configuration here, and how does White make it come about?

Answers

1 After *1* Bf7+ Kxf7 White has no good way to continue the attack. Instead *1* Qxh7+! forces *1* . . . KXh7 when *2* Bf7! is discovered check and mate. Note how the bishop uses its move to control the g8 square.

2 White forces mate with *4* Qxe8+! Kxe8 *5* Rf8+ Ke7 *6* R1f7 mate. The final position is another, rather elaborate variation on the standard two-rooks mate.

3 White played *1* Qh8+!! forcing *1* . . . Kxh8 when *2* Nxf7+ forked King and Queen. After *2* . . . Kg7 or *2* . . . Kg8, White plays *3* Nxg5 remaining a Knight and a Pawn ahead.

04

principles of opening play

In this chapter you will learn:

- how to bring out your pieces at the start of a game
- how to select a battle plan and modify it according to the opponent's moves
- the basic principles of sound and effective development – and when to break them.

Finally we come to the start of the game. Now that we have had some examples of the powers of the various pieces when the White and Black armies clash in hand-to-hand fighting, we must learn how best to organize them into battle formations. The military metaphor is appropriate for a chess game, though with each side fully aware of the other side's deployments, opportunity for surprise commando-type raids is necessarily limited. There is, in fact, a deviant version of chess called 'Kriegspiel' (war-game) in which each player only knows where his own men are, but has various means of discovering information about the opponent's army. Here we are only concerned with pure chess: each player can see his opponent's forces and his opponent's threats – it is a game of complete information.

At the start of the game, each side is firmly restricted to his own half of the board. The mass of White pieces in the back half is ideally placed to repel any Black invasion force. For an attack to be successful, it should be well prepared. And the task during the opening of the game should be to ensure that one's forces are actively positioned and ready to cooperate with one another. Above all, three objectives should be paramount in one's thoughts during the opening phase of the game:

1 development of the pieces
2 control of the centre of the board
3 the conquest of space.

We shall discuss each of these in detail.

Development of the pieces

This means at its simplest bringing the men off the back rank, somewhere into the middle of the board where they might be of more use in threatening the enemy. At the very start of the game, however, one has no idea where the opponent is going to be putting his pieces, and consequently no idea where one's own men will be needed as the game progresses. As the pieces and Pawns are brought into play, the shape of the battle begins to take form. Each move made divulges more of a player's plans, and provides information about where both sides' men will be most aggressively placed. Whichever side secures his own King's safety and mobilizes his other men more quickly will be the first to be in a position to launch an attack, so time is of the essence in the opening.

The principles of development to be remembered are as follows:

- bring all the pieces into play as quickly as possible
- castle early, to bring the Rooks into the game and the King into safety
- try to combine developing moves with attack on the opponent's undefended points
- do not lose time by allowing your pieces to be chased about as your opponent brings out his own men.

Remember too that Bishops need diagonals and Rooks need open files if they are to function effectively. Lines tend to be opened as Pawns advance and are exchanged, so one often has to wait before knowing where the Rooks are going to be most effective. Castling connects the two Rooks and eases their passage towards any file which may become open later in the game. Usually the decisions for Bishops are easier, since any Pawn advance is liable to open diagonals and point the way towards an effective Bishop deployment.

Control of the centre

The 'centre' is defined as the squares e4, d4, e5 and d5, and much of a well-played opening is centred around the struggle for control of those squares. The reason for this is simply understood: the centre is the hub of the chessboard, where attack and defence can meet, and where the King's side of the board rubs shoulders with the Queen's side. If one is to keep lines of communication open, control of the centre is essential. As the pattern of the game develops, it may easily become necessary to shift emphasis from attack to defence, or from one part of the board to another. Centrally placed pieces can move into action on all four corners of the board at a moment's notice, so until priorities become clear, the centre of the board remains the most useful and important area.

Just as one should give the greatest attention to the four squares which form the centre, the 12 squares surrounding them should also be treated with respect. The area bounded by c-file and f-file and by third and sixth ranks has been termed the 'little centre'. With more influence than the edge, and less than the full centre, those squares also form useful bases for pieces where they can maintain some flexibility of action.

Notice that throughout this brief explanation we have only referred to *control* of the centre, rather than occupation. It is more important to secure control of the central squares for use by one's pieces when they need them as transit stops between one half of the board and the other, than actually to occupy those squares too quickly. Occupation may often be a considerable aid towards ultimate gain of control, but as we shall see later, control may also be effected at a distance.

In early computer chess programs, opening strategy was simulated by attaching different values to different squares on the board. By scoring, say, three points each time a piece attacks one of the four centre squares, two points for an attack on any of the twelve little-centre squares, and one point for any other square on the board, the programmer simulates a view of the chessboard in which the edges are less important than the middle. The difficulty for the machine is to recognize when the centre of gravity of play moves from the geometrical centre of the board. A human player knows instinctively to move his pieces towards the sound of gunfire. The centre may only be a useful stopping-off point on that journey of re-deployment.

Until the early manoeuvres are completed, however, the centre is the most important place on the board. The player who controls the centre is well placed to dictate the future course of events and switch play at will from one side to the other.

The conquest of space

The *tactics* of chess are concerned mainly with the gain of material; the *strategy* may be associated with the gain of territory. Knights, Bishops, Queens and Rooks need safe squares from which to operate; equally important is the task of denying the opponent such safe squares for his own pieces. The chessman ideally suited to the job of the conquest of territory is the Pawn, for no piece of larger value dare tread where a Pawn may capture it. While bringing out one's men from the back rank, therefore, the Pawns may also be advanced, preparing safe ground for their later plans.

Achieving the correct balance between Pawn moves and moves of the other pieces in the opening is one of the more difficult problems of early development. Too many Pawn moves, and the opponent will gain time attacking those Pawns; too many piece moves and there is danger of those pieces being chased back by

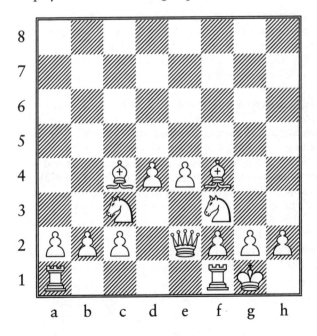

space-gaining Pawn advances of the opponent. The ideal balance is to make just enough Pawn moves to secure squares on which all the pieces can operate without fear of molestation. As we shall see in many examples, the Pawn moves are perhaps the most difficult in chess. Remember that the Pawns cannot move backwards: once a Pawn has renounced its control over a square by advancing, that control can never be regained.

Now let us see how these ideas work out in the formulation of a plan for the opening and the decision of what moves to play. A good idea is to begin the game with a pre-planned scheme of where all one's men will be positioned. That scheme may have to be modified with each move the opponent makes, and the final positions of all the pieces may bear only scant resemblances to the original design, but such a scheme gives something to work towards and helps towards deciding on the individual moves. The diagram on page 68 gives a sensible pattern of development to aim for. This diagram, and the two following, show only White pieces, as they represent a development scheme in White's mind, to be modified according to Black's play. Note the following important features:

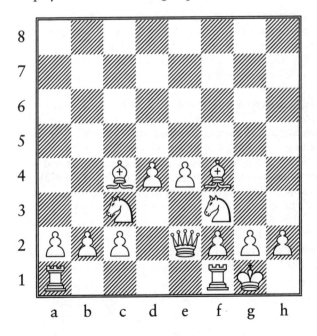

- each piece has moved only once, avoiding loss of time
- all the men are centrally placed, prepared for any eventuality
- the Pawns at d4 and e4 occupy two centre squares and attack the other two at d5 and e5
- the White Rooks are connected and free to occupy a central file when one becomes open after exchanges of Pawns
- finally, the White King is safely castled behind a wall of defensive Pawns and ready to meet any attack.

Now let us look at a sequence of opening moves and see how circumstances cause a modification of White's plans.

1 e4 e5

Already a change of plan is indicated. The Black Pawn covers both d4 and f4, squares which White wanted to utilize. Perhaps it was too much to hope that Black would allow our expansive formation so readily. A little contraction is called for: move the Bishop back from f4 to e3, the Pawn back from d4 to d3 to modify our ideal set-up.

2 Nf3 Nc6

Two functional developing moves; White brings his Knight into the game attacking a Pawn, Black's Knight rushes out to defend it.

3 Bc4 Bc5

Both Bishops are now well-placed on active, open diagonals. It is interesting to observe that the move *1* ... e5 by Black actually contributed to a weakening of the diagonal from a2 to f7. If that Pawn were still on e7, Black could move it to e6, placing a huge obstacle in the path of the White Bishop. Equally, White's *1* e4 could be considered to have lessened White's potential control of the diagonal from f2 to a7. Of course, one would not criticize either Pawn move on those accounts. Any Pawn move will lose control in some direction but gain it in another.

4 0-0 Nf6
5 d3 d6

Black's move attacked the e-Pawn, so White selected a move from his modified plan which defended it; equally *5* Nc3 might have been chosen. Either would fit in with his development scheme.

6 Nc3 0-0
7 Be3

Another move from the plan, but White might also have considered 7 Bg5, a move into the opponent's half of the board, invited by Black's chosen piece formation. Pinning the Knight to Black's Queen, White would restrict his opponent's freedom of action.

7 . . . Bxe3
8 fxe3

We could say here that the opening is satisfactorily concluded. White has brought out his pieces and one more Queen move will leave his Rooks ready for action. The exchange of Bishops has created an open line for the Rook on f1 (the Knight can easily be moved from f3 to allow the Rook full scope) and White can begin to make plans for the middlegame.

The above moves are only given as an example of the formulation, modification and fulfilment of a plan of development for the opening. In a later chapter, we shall have far more to say about opening strategy and about the particular move sequence given above. For the moment, there are some more 'opening principles' which need to be discussed.

Rules and when to break them

Beginners are besieged in chess books such as this with pieces of advice masquerading under the guise of chess principles, yet when they see games of Grandmasters, those principles seem to be broken all the time. Let us then look at some of these 'principles' and discover some of the real ideas which underline them.

Rule 1: Do not bring your Queen out early

The logic of this rule is that the Queen, while a powerful attacking piece, is generally poor at fighting for control of the board. If the Queen is brought into play quickly, she becomes vulnerable to attack by the lighter pieces. Each time she is attacked, time is lost as she moves again.

On the other hand, it must be admitted that a centrally placed Queen does attack a large number of squares. If a central square does become available for the Queen, where she will be free from possibility of attack by enemy men, then she can exert a strong influence. To illustrate this point, we might consider two similar opening sequences:

(a) 1 e4 e5   2 d4 exd4   3 Qxd4
(b) 1 e4 e5   2 Nf3 Nc6   3 d4 exd4   4 Nxd4 Nxd4   5 Qxd4

In the first case, we may criticize White for bringing his Queen out too early. By continuing 3 . . . Nc6, Black brings a piece into the game, on an active square, and forces White to lose time moving his Queen away from attack.

In the second example, White's play is far less open to criticism. The only move which attacks the White Queen safely is 5 . . . c5, a non-developing move which has the added defect of losing permanent control of the d5 square. After 6 Qe3, White can look forward to completing his development with Bc4, Nc3 and later establishing a piece in Black's half of the board on d5.

Returning to the position after 5 Qxd4, Black has another way of threatening the Queen: 5 . . . Ne7 followed by Nc6, but that takes two moves and so in effect loses as much time for Black as for White.

In general it is a mistake to bring out Queens and Rooks, when they will be able to be attacked by lighter pieces moving to effective squares. In doing so, your opponent will be proceeding towards a complete mobilization of his pieces, while your own development will lag behind as the Queen goes roaming alone.

Before leaving this theme, it is appropriate to quote opening moves of a truly terrible game lost by a primitive chessplaying computer program with the White pieces. The machine clearly appreciated the value of the centre squares which it desperately tried to control with its Queen. As an example of why such a strategy is flawed, these moves can hardly be improved upon:

1 e4 e5   2 d4 exd4   3 Qxd4 Nc6   4 Qd5 Nf6   5 Qf5 d5
6 Qf4 Bd6   7 Qg5 h6   8 Qxg7 Rh7. White loses his Queen for the Rook, and still he has no pieces in play. Of course, loss of the Queen was not necessary, but by the time she fell, Black had gained total control of the central squares for which the Queen had been so vainly fighting.

Later in this chapter, we shall examine some less trivial examples of attempts to use the Queen early in the game in an attacking manner.

Rule 2: Do not move a piece more than once in the opening

In principle this ought to be good advice. If one can develop all one's men, moving each once only, then one will be ready for action more quickly than an opponent who potters about with each man, changing his mind about where it should stand. But let us look at a couple of sequences of opening moves:

(a) 1 e4 e5   2 Nf3 Nc6   3 Bb5 a6   4 Ba4 Nf6   5 0-0 b5   6 Bb3;
(b) 1 e4 Nf6   2 e5 Nd5   3 c4 Nb6   4 d4 d6.

The first of these examples sees the White Bishop moving three times within the first six moves, yet it is one of the most popular ways of beginning a game. The second sequence is also not uncommon, but Black's Knight has made three moves before anything else joins in the game at all. The key to understanding such play lies in looking at what the opponent is doing in each case. In neither example does the other player bring out any pieces while the moves are 'being wasted' by moving the same man. Both are examples of using repeated moves of one piece to lure forward the enemy Pawns, in the hope that those Pawns will be vulnerable later, or that their advances will leave areas of weakness behind them. Such a strategy is quite sophisticated (especially in example b, where Black actually invites the White Pawns to dominate the centre), but not as illogical as it may seem.

Rule 3: Knights before Bishops

In bygone days this was an oft-quoted rule of development, based on the idea that Knights could usually be relied upon to develop on f3, c3, f6 and c6, whereas it was usually advisable to wait until later before deciding where the Bishops would be at their most effective. There is, however, no inherent logic to the rule, except in positions where one is indeed confident that the Knight will be well placed on those squares. In many modern opening systems, the role of the Bishop is decided first, then everything is done to ensure that its diagonal is kept free and uncluttered. What is good advice, however, is to play those moves essential to one's development plan before adding the optional extras.

Flexibility is the key to successful development, so options should be left open where possible.

In short, then, the only rule which really does pertain to opening play is the one which advises getting one's pieces into active play as quickly as possible. Delay is only permitted either to take advantage of an error by the opponent or to induce a comparable delay in the opponent's development plans.

We have already examined one sequence of opening moves (pp. 68–9) in which White began with an ideal position for his pieces, then had to modify that ideal as Black's moves appeared on the board. Of course, there are very many possible development schemes which one may adopt as ideal. Before ending this brief discussion of the opening, let us look at two more of the vast number of acceptable schemes of development, just to give an idea of what one should be thinking about when bringing out the pieces.

Remember always that the scheme of development should be determined within the first few moves. It will undergo constant modification, but the plans will only be scrapped if tactical circumstances of such overwhelming importance arise that instant action is demanded.

The following two positions illustrate widely differing patterns of pieces, but both fully conform with our principles: the pieces are brought into play, Kings castled into safety, and the centre of the board is kept under close surveillance. Such a pattern of pieces is described as an *opening system* and the most important systems have names attached to them, usually the names of their originators or of the great players who first gave popularity to the system.

In the development plan on page 73, White has been realistically modest in his aims. He has a firm foothold in the centre, with the d-Pawn strongly supported. White's pieces put in a good claim for control of e4 and e5, both Bishops have good diagonals and the Queen is ready to play to c2 or e2 putting her weight behind the white-squared Bishop. The h3 Pawn move is an interesting accessory: in the long term, it may serve to provide the King an escape square on h2 in case of a back-rank

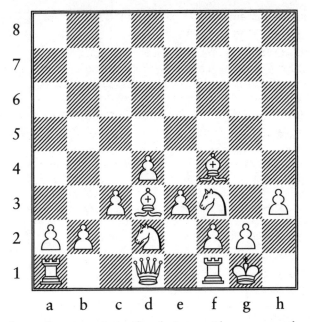

mate threat, but more immediately it provides a retreat for the Bishop on f4. By playing e3 after Bf4, White has cut off its retreat in one direction. Normally one would be reluctant to play such a move as h3, just in case the Bishop needed a retreat, but such a move can often turn out to be an indispensable part of an opening scheme. Note also how White has tended to develop his pieces behind his central Pawns, leaving those Pawns free to advance and gain space later in the game. The order of White's moves might easily have been d4, Nf3, Bf4, e3, Bd3, 0-0, Nbd2, h3, c3. Alternatively, White could have opted for a more aggressive plan with c4 and Nc3 in place of the restrained c3 and Nbd2; again the Knight develops behind the Pawn to facilitate its later advance.

The next position illustrates a completely different, but equally valid approach to the problem of development in the opening.

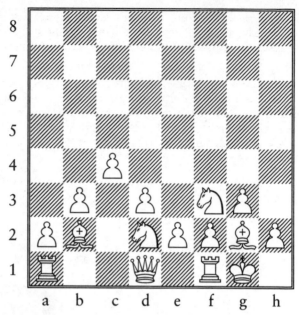

Here the essential feature is the development of the Bishops. Placing them at b2 and g2, they are on their longest diagonals and their influence has not been interrupted by putting Pawns at d4 or e4. The Knight on f3 lessens the immediate power of the g2-Bishop, but its strength may be felt since the Knight is fully able to move away and uncover the Bishop whenever it chooses. White's Pawns on d3 and c4, controlling e4 and d5 respectively, enhance the prospects of the white-squared Bishop. The Knight on f3 and Bishop on b2 both add their weight to control of d4 and e5. So although White has been more reticent in advancing his centre Pawns, the theme of his development structure is still very much one of central control.

The structure on the White's King's side is very commonly seen in modern chess. It is known as a *fianchetto* development of the Bishop (from the Italian, meaning 'little flank'). By extension, any development of a Bishop to g2 or b2 (g7 or b7 in Black's case) is called a fianchetto of the Bishop.

The attack on f7

We have already met two drastically short games: scholar's mate (p.56) and fool's mate (p. 54). In the first, White attacked f7 with Bishop and Queen; Black missed the point and allowed

Qxf7 mate on move four. In fool's mate, White lost in two moves by advancing f-Pawn and g-Pawn to allow Qh4 mate. These quick games share a common theme – the weakness of the f-Pawn.

The square on which the f-Pawn starts the game, and the diagonal connecting the Pawn with its King, are the most vulnerable areas in early play. Many games are won by single-minded attacks on f7 or f2, but they ought not to be. With so many pieces clustered round the King, it takes a degree of carelessness for the defender to fall foul of such quick attacks. Let us look more closely as some possible continuations if White's immediate attack is met by sensible defence. We shall begin with the opening moves of scholar's mate:

1 e4 e5   2 Bc4 Bc5   3 Qh5

White attacks e5 and f7, so Black must find a move to protect both those Pawns:

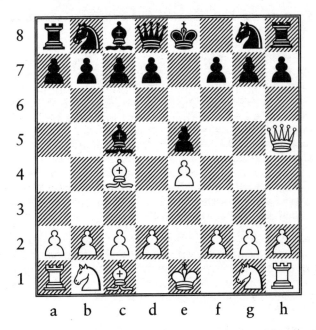

3 . . . Qe7

Equally, Black might choose *3 . . . Qf6* attacking f2 himself. After *3 . . . Qe7*, Black can look forward to gaining time with

Nf6, attacking the White Queen. After, for example, 4 Nc3 (hoping to attack the Black Queen with Nd5) 4 . . . Nf6 5 Qg5 0-0 Black's development is well advanced. 6 Nd5? would even lose a piece to 6 . . . Nxd5 (discovering an attack on the Queen) 7 Qxe7 Nxe7.

Instead of 4 Nc3, it is more interesting to examine the consequences of 4 Nf3. White attacks e5 and even prepares another attack on f7 with Ng5. We might consider a number of continuations:

(a) 4 . . . Nf6 5 Qxe5 Nxe4 6 Qxe7+ Bxe7 and White's 'attack' has led only to an exchange of Queens;

(b) 4 . . . Nc6 5 Ng5 Nd8 6 Nxh7? (Better 6 0-0 or 6 Nc3) g6! 7 Qh3 d5! attacking Bishop and Queen and winning a piece at least. Note in this sequence how 6 . . . g6 defended against the threat of Nf6+ by opening the line between f6 and h8 and ensuring that Qxf6 would defend the Black Rook.

(c) 4 . . . d6 5 Ng5 Nh6 6 Nc3 c6 (keeping the Knight out of d5) 7 0-0 Nd7 8 d3 Nf6 9 Qh4 d5 10 exd5 Nf5! 11 Qh3 (the only safe square) 11 . . . Ne3! (discovering an attack on the Queen) 12 Qf3 (12 Qh4 is better, when Black has the choice from 12 . . . Nxf1, 12 . . . Nxd5 or repeating position with 12 . . . Nf5) 12 . . . Bg4 13 Qg3 Nf5 and the White Queen has nowhere to run. Of course, that was a rather drastic example of punishment for early Queen development, but typical of the sort of mess liable to happen when an optimistic Queen sortie is followed by further inaccuracy.

The characteristic defences to f7 were all illustrated in those variations: Qe7 or Qf6, Nh6, and 0-0 are the most usual ways to protect f7, with Nd8 (retreating from c6) a less common resource from the defensive armoury. Now let us examine a more subtle way to attack the f-Pawn, not with Queen and Bishop, but with Bishop and Knight. The following opening moves are very common:

1 e4 e5
2 Nf3 Nc6
3 Bc4

The Bishop is already bearing down on the vulnerable Pawn and the Knight stands ready to add his weight from g5 if Black allows it. (That square, of course, is defended by the Queen at the moment.)

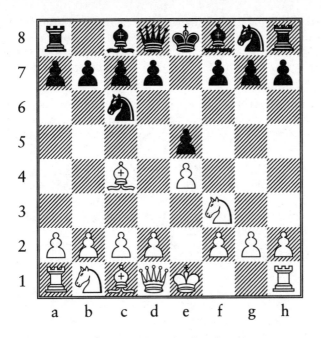

Now Black has a number of perfectly adequate moves: *3 . . . Be7, 3 . . . Bc5* or *3 . . . d6* all conform to opening principles (though the last of these lets out one Bishop at the expense of blocking a path for the other). The natural developing move *3 . . . Nf6* is a little incautious, however, since it has the effect of blocking the Queen's view of g5. White can now play *4 Ng5* and Black has none of his normally available defences to f7: he cannot yet castle, and his Queen is too heavy a defender – after *4 . . . Qe7 5 Bxf7+*, Black would come off far worse from the exchanges on f7. The only move to counter the attack on f7 is to block the Bishop's diagonal with *4 . . . d5*. Let us see how that came to grief in an 1858 game won by Paul Morphy:

5 exd5 Nxd5

Surprisingly, a mistake; Black should attack the Bishop with *5 . . . Na5* and later chase the Knight with h6. He may never regain his Pawn, but he drives back the attackers and gains much time. In this manner *3 . . . Nf6* becomes a playable move after all.

6 d4!

White plays to mobilize his forces as quickly as possible. Instead *6 Qf3 Qxg5 7 Bxd5 Nd8* or in this line *7 Qxd5 Be6* would have got White nowhere. The tempting continuation was 6 Nxf7 Kxf7 7 Qf3+, forcing the Black King to e6 if he wants to save the Knight on d5. Morphy's idea is based on the same theme.

6 ... exd4
7 0-0 Be7 (see diagram)

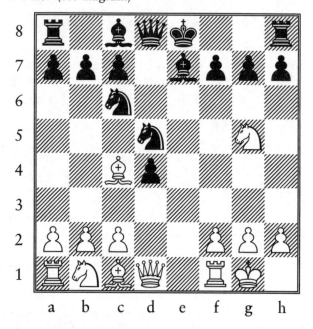

Given one more move, Black would castle out of danger. White's whole theme has been to attack the King in the centre. His next move invests a Knight to keep the monarch under fire.

8 Nxf7! Kxf7
9 Qf3+ Ke6

Otherwise White will simply regain his piece with 10 Bxd5

10 Nc3!

This new investment is to open more lines of attack and allow the a1-Rook to join in without delay.

10 ... dxc3
11 Re1+ Ne5
12 Bf4 Bf6

White utilizes the power of his pins very instructively. Now follows a demolition job to complete the exposure of the Black King:

> **13 Bxe5 Bxe5**
> **14 Rxe5+! Kxe5**
> **15 Re1+ Kd4**

15 . . . Kd6 16 Qxd5 would already be checkmate.

> **16 Bxd5 Re8**

16 . . . Qxd5 would have allowed *17 Qxc3* mate, but Black's King has been forced too far away from home for the defenders to come to his aid against the attacking force of Queen, Rook and Bishop.

> **17 Qd3+ Kc5**
> **18 b4+ Kxb4**
> **19 Qd4+**

And Black is mated whichever way he runs: *19 . . . Ka5 20 Qxc3+ Ka6 21 Qa3+ Kb5 (or b6) 22 Rb1* mate; or *19 . . . Ka5 20 Qxc3+ Ka4 21 Qb3+ Ka5 22 Qa3+ Kb6 (or b5) 23 Rb1* mate; or *19 . . . Kb5 20 Rb1+ Ka5 21 Qb4+ Ka6 22 Qb5* mate; or *19 . . . Ka3 20 Qxc3+ Ka4 21 Qb3+* as before. With nowhere to hide the Black King is quickly gunned down in the wide open spaces. The reader should be able to work out some other mates for himself.

That game should be enough to demonstrate the importance of castling early in the game as well as showing how a lead in development can be exploited dramatically if the position is sufficiently open.

05

endgame strategy

In this chapter you will learn:
- the distinction between tactics and strategy
- the importance, especially when few pieces remain on the board, of formulating a plan and carrying it out patiently and systematically
- to appreciate how good chess is a subtle interplay of good planning (strategy) and accurate calculation (tactics).

In the early part of this book, we have concentrated on the elements of chess tactics: winning pieces, delivering checkmate, punishing errors. These are the elements which must be kept under control if the higher reaches of chess thought are to have scope to function. For the remainder of the book, we shall be discovering more about chess strategy: the art of planning ahead in order to obtain those positions where the tactics will be likely to decide matters in one's favour.

The chess strategist thinks in terms of plans rather than single moves. He decides how he would like his position to improve over the next few moves, he sets sub-goals, then begins to think about how to reach those end points.

We have already looked at some of the basic endgames. Now we shall look at some endgames with more pieces on the board, in which the role of planning ahead will become clear.

The endgame is a rather imprecise term in chess. Nobody has successfully managed to define where a middlegame ends and an endgame begins. If one wants a definition, the principal characteristic of the endgame is that the King can come out into the open without great fear of being mated, and can be active in helping the fulfilment of one's plans. To say that the endgame begins when Queens are exchanged is too much a simplification. The other pieces are perfectly well able to combine in a mating attack without the aid of the Queen.

In the endgame, a single extra Pawn can be enough to decide the outcome, as we have indeed already seen with positions in which King and Pawn win against King. The first positions we shall discuss in this chapter are King and Pawn endgames (each side having a King and the only other men on the board being Pawns).

We begin with a typical position in which White has an extra Pawn (see diagram overleaf). White to play:

A quick count verifies that the a-Pawn can be stopped by the Black King if it races towards the queening square: 1 a5 Kd7 2 a6 Kc7 3 a7 Kb7 4 a8=Q+ Kxa8.

There is a simple geometrical way to see if a King can stop such a Pawn: construct a square, two of the corners of which are the Pawn and the queening square. If the defending King is inside the square it can stop the Pawn; if it is outside, the Pawn wins the race. In this case the square is bounded by a4, a8, e8, e4 and Black's King is just inside. (If a Pawn is on the second rank, the square has to be drawn as if it were on the third, to allow for the double-move.)

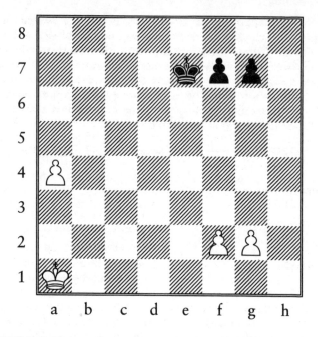

So if White's Pawn cannot win on its own, the King must help. Now we know that King and a-Pawn cannot win against lone King in such a position, but the Pawns on the other side of the board make all the difference. The winning strategy is to use the extra Pawn to lure the Black King over to the Q-side, then at an appropriate moment to make a dash for the other wing and exploit his absence by attacking the Pawns over there. *1 Kb2 Kd6 2 Kb3 Kc5 3 Kc3 Kb6 4 Kb4 Ka6 5 a5 Kb7* (or *5 . . . g6 6 g3* and Black quickly runs out of Pawn moves and has to move his King anyway) *6 Kc5* (now is as good a time as any to rush to the other wing) *6 . . . Ka6* (Black must eliminate the a-Pawn before he can even think of moving his King towards the K-side) *7 Kd6 Kxa5 8 Ke7 f5 9 Kf7 g5 10 Kf6* and White's King will capture both Black Pawns long before the Black King has a chance to influence matters. White's subsequent win with two Pawns against none is then simple.

The creation of passed Pawns

The White a-Pawn in that starting position could exert a powerful effect because it had a free path to the queening square, unhampered by an enemy Pawn. Such a Pawn, with no enemy Pawn on its own file, or on either of the neighbouring files able to capture it if it advances, is called a **passed Pawn**. Most of the strategy of endgames is concerned with the formation of passed Pawns and what to do with them when you have them. The technique exemplified above is absolutely typical: a passed Pawn on one wing is used mainly for its diversionary value. Its threat of becoming a Queen forces the enemy King away from the other side of the board, leaving the Pawns on that wing vulnerable to attack at a moment of White's choosing. We shall see later that exactly the same technique is appropriate even when there are other pieces besides Kings and Pawns on the board.

In general the technique for winning with an extra Pawn is to create a passed Pawn, then push it forward until enemy forces are occupied with preventing it from queening, then exploiting their absence in another area of the board. In a King and Pawn endgame, such a technique ought to bring victory, unless the circumstances are exceptional. The attacking King will always win the race to the other side by at least two moves. And he will have the advantage of his King in front of his own Pawns when he has eliminated the enemy Pawns. We may state then that, in general, if there are many Pawns on the board, a single Pawn advantage in a King and Pawn endgame is sufficient to win.

The next diagram shows an example of 'exceptional circumstances' which may upset the normal course of events.

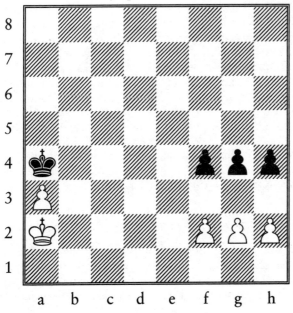

White must play with care: the seemingly natural 1 Kb2 actually loses after *1 . . . g3! 2* hxg3 f3! *3* gxf3 h3 and Black queens a Pawn long before White. Equally *1 . . . g3 2* fxg3 h3! *3 gxh3 f3* has the same result. Black creates a winning passed Pawn in these variations by a massive breakthrough. Instead White must begin with *1* g3! hxg3 *2* hxg3 or *1 . . . fxg3 2* fxg3, keeping the Pawns blocked on that wing and guaranteeing ultimate victory.

The unusual feature of this example is that Black managed to create a passed Pawn as it were out of nothing. Three Black Pawns face three White Pawns and it is surprising that one can force its way through.

Normally an advantage of one Pawn on either wing is enough to force the creation of a passed Pawn. We shall examine the technique of creating passed Pawns in the context of King and Pawn endgames, but the method translates exactly to any other endgame. When one side has more Pawns on one wing than his opponent, he is said to have a **Pawn majority** on that wing. Out of that Pawn majority it will normally be possible to create a passed Pawn, but the Pawns have to be advanced in precise manner, as we shall see. The diagram opposite is a more complex example of the same type of position as seen before. White has a Pawn majority on the Q-side, but not yet a passed Pawn. His first task is to create one.

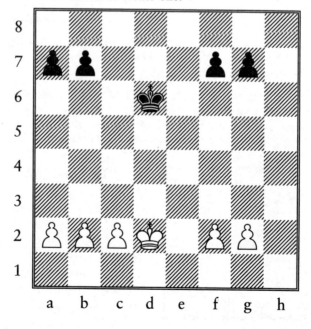

1 c4!

The correct Pawn to advance first is almost always the Pawn which has no opposite number on its file. If instead White had played *1* b4? then after *1* . . . b5! he finds his majority blocked. He can try *2* Kd3, but *2* . . . Kd5! keeps control of c4 and maintains restraint on the White Pawn advance. Equally *1* a4 a5! *2* c3 Kc5 makes it difficult for White to advance his Pawns.

1 . . . Kc5
2 Kc3 a5
3 b3!

Instead *3* a3 a4! would make life much more difficult for White. After *4* b4+ axb3 e.p. *5* Kxb3, Black's one remaining Q-side Pawn holds up both the White ones. White might still be able to win, but the task would be made more complex.

3 . . . b6
4 a3! g6
5 b4+ axb4
6 axb4+ Kc6
7 Kd4

After patient preparation, White is finally ready to advance c5 and create a passed Pawn. The rest of the endgame is the same routine which we have met before: *7* . . . Kd6 *8* c5+ bxc5 *9* bxc5+ Kc6 *10* Kc4 Kc7 *11* Kd5 Kd7 *12* Ke5 Kc6 (or *12* . . . Ke7 *13* c6) *13* Kf6 Kxc5 *14* Kxf7 and White wins comfortably.

This manner of advancing the White Pawns systematically to prevent their being held up by the opposition is an essential part of the technique of endgame play.

Before leaving this example, let us return to the position at the third move and see just how White does still manage to win after playing the inferior *3* a3 a4 *4* b4+ axb3 e.p. *5* Kxb3. The technique here is also instructive (see diagram). White must be prepared to return his extra Pawn:

5 . . . b6 *6* Kc3 g5
7 g4 f6 *8* f3 Kc6
9 Kd4 Kd6 *10* a4 Kc6
11 c5! (*11* Ke4 Kd6
12 Kf5 Ke7 is less convincing)
11 . . . bxc5+
12 Kc4 Kb6 *13* Kd5 Ka5
14 Kxc5 Kxa4 *15* Kd6 Kb4
16 Ke6 and again

White has won the race to the K-side Pawns. The White c-Pawn in this play was used as a decoy, luring the Black b-Pawn one file towards the centre of the board, with the result that White's a-Pawn became a passed Pawn demanding the attention of the Black King. Black's own passed Pawn on c5 has curiously little effect on the action which followed its creation. What was crucial here was that the White passed Pawn, on the a-file, was further away from the K-side Pawns than Black's on the c-file. Thus, after both Pawns had been captured, the Black King ended up stranded, too far away from the subsequent play. A Pawn such as White's a-Pawn in the latter stage of this endgame, is sometimes called an *Outside* (or *Distant*) *Passed Pawn*.

In general, a player with more Pawns on one wing should be able to create a passed Pawn by systematically advancing those Pawns in the manner described. Sometimes, however, if more than one Pawn is on the same file, a Pawn majority can become useless.

Two Pawns of the same colour standing on the same file (after one has made a capture) are known as **doubled Pawns** and their existence can considerably reduce their effectiveness in an endgame.

Black to play holds up the Pawns: 1 ... c5 2 c4+ Ke5 3 c3 b6 4 b4 Kf5 and White has no way to persuade Black to capture on b4. 5 Kc2 Ke4 6 Kb3 Kd3 could even lose for White.

The doubled Pawns here completely lose the effectiveness of White's Pawn majority.

We have already seen how, in King and Pawn endgames, precision can be essential in choosing the right square for the King each move. To be at the right place at the right time when the opponent's King threatens to penetrate can demand exact play many moves before that time arrives. The most innocuous looking positions can contain subtle finesses. Whole books have been written on the theory of King and Pawn endings; there is space here for only a few more examples. Firstly, a justly celebrated endgame study composed by Richard Reti. The diagram below shows the starting position, with White to play. It looks impossible to stop the Black Pawn from queening, or to have much hope of reaching the eighth rank with White's Pawn, but by precise King moves, White can save the game. The key to this position lies in the knowledge that on the chessboard the shortest distance between two points may as well be a zig-zag as a straight line.

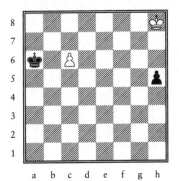

White draws with
1 Kg7 h4   2 Kf6 h3
3 Ke7 h2   4 c7 Kb7
5 Kd7 and White queens his Pawn too. Or
1 Kg7 h4   2 Kf6 Kb6
3 Ke5 h3 (3 . . . Kxc6
4 Kf4 catches the Pawn)
4 Kd6 h2   5 c7 and again White's Pawn is shepherded home to equalize the game.

The second diagram illustrates another type of finesse based on the idea of 'the opposition' or 'related squares'. Black to play loses this position, but if it is White's move the correct result is a draw. White's plan is based on outflanking the enemy King and attacking and winning the Pawn on f5. For example (Black playing first) 1 . . . Kd6   2 Kd4 Ke6   3 Kc5 Kf6   4 Kd5 Kf7   5 Ke5 Kg6   6 Ke6 and the f-Pawn is lost. Other first moves for Black also lose: 1 . . . Ke6   2 Kc4! Kd6   3 Kd4 reaches the same position (but not 2 Kd4? Kd6! when Black keeps the White King at bay). Finally 1 . . . Kc5 allows White to reach a winning King-and-Pawn against King position with 2 e4!

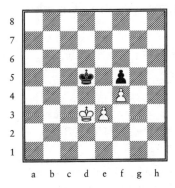

fxe4+ 3 Kxe4 and 4 Kf5! when the King in front of the Pawn ensures its coronation on f8.

Now let us study the same position with White moving first. After *1 Kc3 Kc5! 2 Kc2 Kc6! 3 Kd2 Kd6! 4 Kd3 Kd5*, Black can ensure that it is never his move when the diagram position is reached. It is almost always a mistake for Black to play the 'aggressive' Ke4 (unless he can be sure of taking the e-Pawn on his following move). For example, *1 Kc3 Ke4? 2 Kd2 Kf3 (2 . . . Kd5 3 Kd3! and Black must move and lose) 3 Kd3 Kf2 4 Kd4 Kf3 5 Ke5 Kg4 6 Kf6* and the f-Pawn is doomed.

White can try a more subtle winning attempt with *1 Kc2*, but Black holds the game by playing *1 . . . Kc6! 2 Kd2 Kd6!*, never going to d5 or c5 until White's King treads on the corresponding square of d3 or c3.

We could in fact move the Black King to d7 in the original position without changing our assessment. Again, White to play cannot win since *1 Kd4 Kd6 2 Kc4 Kc6* always keeps his King at bay. The best White can do is reach a drawn King-and-Pawn against King position.

Techniques of winning with an extra Pawn

Many of the principles of King and Pawn endgames apply equally to endgames in which other pieces also feature. In particular, when there are many Pawns on the board, the winning process may frequently be divided into two stages: the creation of a passed Pawn, followed by the advance of that Pawn to divert enemy forces away from defensive duties on the opposite wing. We shall see examples of this process with Rooks, Bishops and Knights in addition to the Pawns. In such endgames a single extra Pawn is often enough to win the game, but the prospects of victory tend to be greater the more Pawns there are on the board. The reason for this is simple: after the creation of a passed Pawn, and the use of the threat of that Pawn's advance to divert the enemy forces, the more Pawns left unprotected on the other wing, the larger the harvest when they are eventually reaped by an invading force.

The material which follows is arranged according to the type of pieces remaining on the board. As we shall see, many of the same principles apply throughout endgame theory. The differing nature of the pieces, however, introduces further subtleties.

Bishop and Pawn endgames

What makes the Bishop quite different from any other piece is its inability to control certain squares on the board; a white-squared Bishop can never reach the black squares, while the white squares are out of bounds for the black-squared Bishop. This fact is responsible for a whole range of apparently anomalous endgames.

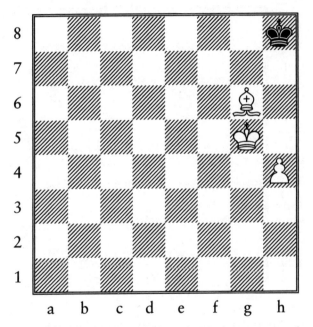

This is the endgame commonly known as the 'wrong-coloured Rook's Pawn' (though actually it is the Bishop which is the wrong colour). White cannot force a win because his Bishop can never control h8. For example, *1* h5 Kg8 *2* h6 Kh8 *3* Bf7 Kh7 *4* Kh5 Kh8 *5* Bg6 (*5* Kg6 is stalemate) Kg8 *6* h7+ Kg7 *7* Kg5 Kh8 *8* Kf5 Kg7, and so on. White can never approach nearer with his King without giving stalemate. With a black-squared Bishop, however, the initial position is an easy win. Starting with the Bishop on h6 instead of g6, White wins

with *1* h5 Kh7 *2* Bf8 Kg8 *3* Bd6 Kh7 *4* h6 Kh8
5 Be5+ Kg8 *6* Kg6 with h7 and h8=Q to follow. In fact,
unless immediate loss of the Pawn is inevitable, it may be said
that Bishop and Pawn should always win against lone King
except for the single case of an a-Pawn or h-Pawn of which the
queening square cannot be controlled by the Bishop.

When both sides have Bishops, a normal winning procedure for
a player with more Pawns can be made considerably more
difficult if the defender's Bishop operates on opposite-coloured
squares from that of the attacker. These so-called 'opposite-
coloured Bishop endgames' are notorious for their drawing
potential.

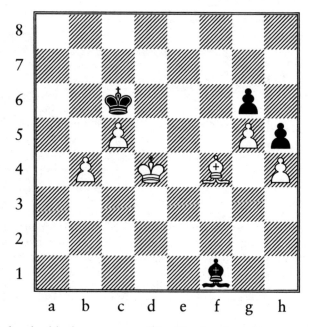

You take the black squares and I will take the white squares.
Even with two extra Pawns, White has no real chances to win
this endgame, because he can make no progress beyond the
white-square blockade which Black has erected. *1* Ke5 Bd3 *2*
Kf6 Kb5 *3* Ke6 Kc6 *4* Kf7 Kb5 and there is nothing for
White to do. Put White's c-Pawn on c3 in the initial position,
however, and he has every chance of victory by preventing such
a blockade: *1* c4 Be2 *2* b5+ Kb6 *3* Bd6 Bf1 *4* Kc3 Be2

5 Kb4 Bd3 *6* c5+ Kb7 *7* c6+ Kb6 *8* Bc5+ Kc7
9 Be7 Kb6 *10* Bd8+ Ka7 *11* Kc5 Be4 *12* b6+ Kb8 *13*
Bc7+ Kc8 *14* Bf4 with b7 and b8=Q to follow. Note how
White tries to keep his Pawns controlling the white squares to
avoid the blockade seen in the earlier example. Only in this
manner can their successful advance be secured.

As a final example related to this theme, let us see what happens
if we remove the K-side Pawns from the position:

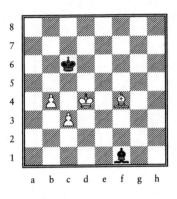

Despite his two-Pawn
advantage, White can no
longer force a win:
1 c4 Be2 *2* b5+ Kb6
3 Bd6 Bg4 *4* Kc3 Bd7
5 Kb4 Be8 *6* c5+ Kb7
and White can make no more
progress since *7* c6+ Bxc6 *8*
bxc6+ Kxc6 leaves only King
and Bishop against King,
which cannot mate. Even a
single Pawn remaining on the
K-side would guarantee
victory to White in this final
position, so Black's defence of giving up the Bishop would not
have saved him in our earlier examples. The important feature
of Black's defensive play in this variation was the placing of the
Bishop on the diagonal from a4–e8, guarding both the b5 and
c6 squares. After the moves *6* c5+ Kb7, the Bishop attacks the
b5-Pawn, tying White's King to its defence and preventing the
White monarch from hurrying to d6 to aid the advance of the
other Pawn to c6. After *7* Ka5 or *7* Kc4, Black patiently waits
with *7* ... Bd7 and can happily oscillate the Bishop between d7
and e8 until it has its chance to give itself up for both Pawns.

When opposing Bishops operate on the same colour squares, the
duel becomes more intense. In general, a player having an extra
Pawn can hope to win by the usual process of creating a passed
Pawn and pushing it. The crucial positions arise when only a
few Pawns remain on the board and the defence has possibilities
of surrendering the Bishop to leave, as in earlier examples, only
King and Bishop against King. Let us consider some typical
positions which have reduced to just Bishop and Pawn against
Bishop.

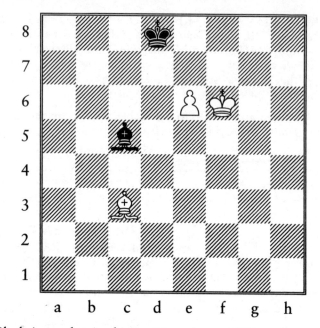

If Black is to play in this position, *1 . . . Ke8!* removes any danger of losing. The King stands on a white square from which it can never be ejected. Black will simply move his Bishop to and fro for as long as White persists in continuing the game. With White to play, however, the story is quite different. After *1 Kf7!* Black's King is kept out of the crucial e8 square. *1 . . . Ba3* (note that *1 . . . Be7?* would lose to *2 Bf6! Bxf6 3 Kxf6 Ke8 4 e7* and White wins) *2 Bg7! Bb4 3 Bf8* and Black can no longer maintain control of the e7 square. He must either exchange Bishops or surrender the f8–a3 diagonal.

That process was simple for White, and the idea involved was one basic to the principles of many such endgames. By offering the exchange of pieces by *3 Bf8*, White gave his opponent the option of a lost King-and-Pawn endgame or the surrender of an important diagonal. The threat of transposition into a winning King-and-Pawn endgame lies at the basis of the theory of how to win endgames with an extra Pawn.

Let us move on to a more complex example of Bishop and Pawn against Bishop to see how such a process may need to be repeated before a successful result is reached.

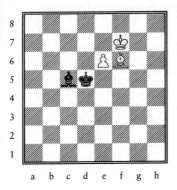

White wins by hounding the enemy Bishop off first one diagonal, then another:

1 Be7 Bf2
2 Ba3 Bh4
3 Bb2 followed by
4 Bf6 and Black cannot maintain his guard on the crucial e7 square.

By offering exchanges on e7 and f6, White forces the Black Bishop out of the way. Note that in this position the plan of **1 Bg7** followed by **2 Bf8** no longer works, since Black can simply take the Bishop when it arrives at f8; White's King has a duty to defend the e-Pawn, so cannot give up its post to recapture on f8.

We need only make a slight change to the position and White is unable to win at all. The lower diagram is only a draw:

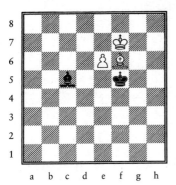

1 Be7 Bf2
2 Ba3 Bh4
3 Bb2 Bg5

White can no longer oppose Bishops with Bf6, so Black's Bishop maintains its post on the d8–h4 diagonal:

4 Bg7 Bh4
5 Bh6 Bd8
6 Bf8 Bg5
7 Be7 Be3
8 Bf6 Bc5 and we are back to the beginning. If White tries **9 Bd4**, or any similar Bishop sacrifice, Black must not be tempted (**9 . . . Bxd4?** **10 e7** wins for White): the Black Bishop must resolutely refuse to be distracted from its duty to watch the e7 square. **9 . . . Ba3!** continues with the merry-go-round.

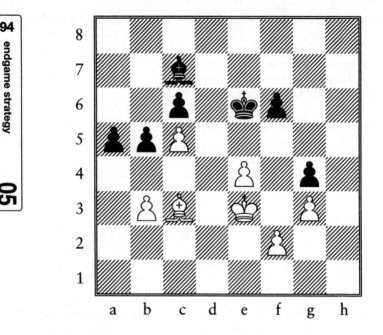

Finally an example of a Bishop-and-Pawn endgame with many Pawns on the board. This position is taken from a game Tchigorin–Pillsbury, London 1899. Although material is level, Black has two distinct advantages in the position. Firstly, he has the possibility to create a distant passed Pawn on the a-file; and secondly, the White Pawns on c5, f2 and g3 are fixed on black squares where they are liable to attack from the Bishop. Small though such advantages sound, they prove decisive. The game concluded *1* Kd3 a4 *2* bxa4 bxa4 *3* Bb4 Be5 *4* Ba3 Ba1! (vacating e5 for the King) *5* Bc1 f5! (the Pawn on e4 keeps Black's King out of d5; it must be exchanged) *6* Ba3 Ke5 *7* exf5 Kxf5 *8* Ke3 Ke5 *9* f4+ (if White does nothing, Black wins simply with Bd4+ and Kd5 followed by Bxc5) *9* . . . Kd5 *10* f5 Be5 *11* Kf2 Ke4 and White resigned. Next move Black takes the f-Pawn, then brings his King back to e4 and over towards the Q-side to shepherd the a-Pawn home. White's King cannot defend both the g-Pawn and the threatened invasion of the other wing.

There is one final variation worth attention before leaving this endgame. Suppose after *1* Kd3 a4 *2* bxa4 bxa4 White had immediately run towards the a-Pawn with his King: *3 Kc4 Be5!* and now *4 Bxe5 Kxe5 5 Kb4 Kxe4 6 Kxa4 Kd4 7 Kb4 Kd5*. Black wins the c-Pawn, then wins the King-and-Pawn ending in the normal fashion. Alternatively *4 Bd2 Bb2 5 Kb4 a3 6 Kb3 Ke5* is just as hopeless; Black captures on e4, then follows with Bd4, harvesting the white Pawns.

Knight- and Pawn-endgames

Though approximately equal in value to a Bishop, the Knight is quite different in character and nowhere does this difference become more apparent than in the endgame. The Bishop moves quickly, but can never influence half the squares on the board. The Knight is slow, ponderous and most effective at short range, but given time it can arrive at any square eventually. The worst qualities of the Knight are illustrated by the position of the diagram.

White to play wins with *1 h6*. The Knight's poor manoeuvrability prevents it from controlling h7 or h8 in time to stop the Pawn. Even *1 . . . Kf8* (or Kf7) would be met by *2 h7* and *3 h8=Q*. Strangely, Black would draw easily if his Knight were absent from the board. Another point to note here is that this phenomenon occurs only with a- or h-Pawn. Move everything one file to the left and *1 g6* is well met by *1 . . . Nh6* guarding the important g8 square.

The Knight's inability to lose a move (the black–white alternation of its squares imposes a parity upon its movements) can lead to some anomalous endgame positions. White to play in the diagram overleaf would win easily with *1 Ng7+*, interfering with the Bishop's duty of guarding h8. Apparently Black cannot prevent Ng7 even if it is his move, yet Black to play can draw the game by a remarkable device: *1 . . . Bh8!* After *2 Kxh8 Kf7! 3 Nf6 Kf8!* nothing can prevent the Black King from oscillating for ever between f7 and f8. White's Knight is always guarding the wrong square.

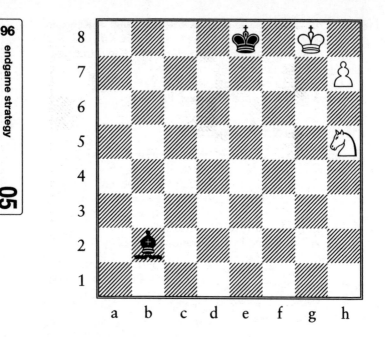

Similarly, after *1* . . . Bh8! *2* Ng7+ Ke7 *3* Nf5+ Ke8, the best White can do is *4* Nh4 Ba1! (not *4* . . . Ke7? *5* Ng6+ winning with *6* Nxh8) *5* Ng6 Bb2 *6* Nf8 Bc3 *7* Ne6 Bh8! and *8* Kxh8 Kf7, which leaves us with the same curious drawn position.

Normally, King, Knight and Pawn against King should be a win, with the Knight and Pawn escorting the Pawn through to the queening square. The only case where a modicum of care is required is with a- or h-Pawn, when some possibilities of stalemate can arise if the Pawn is pushed too quickly to the seventh rank. The next diagram illustrates some of the ideas.

After *1* h6+ Kh8, White must be careful and above all patient. Any King move would give an immediate draw by stalemate, while the over-hasty *2* h7 would also throw away the win. After that move, White's Knight is tied to the defence of the h-Pawn and the Black King moves between g7 and h8. Any approach of the White King (to g6, h6, f7 or f8) will give stalemate. White can make no further progress. The correct way to play is more circumspect: *1* h6+ Kh8 *2* Ne8 Kh7 *3* Nd6 Kg8 *4* Kg6 Kh8 *5* Nf7+ Kg8 *6* h7+ and the Pawn queens next move. Alternatively *1* h6+ Kh8 *2* Ne8 Kg8 *3* Kg6 Kh8 *4* Nd6

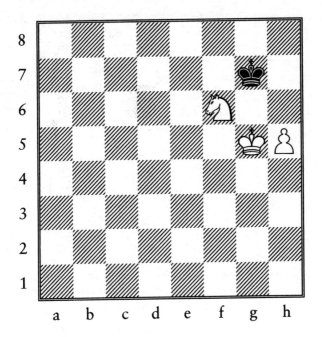

Kg8 5 h7+ Kh8 6 Nf7 mate. In both these lines White simply makes the best use of his resources with the Pawn covering the g8 square at the same times as the Knight covers h8. With all the time in the world at his disposal, White is playing the endgame of King and h-Pawn against King, with the huge additional benefit of a piece which can deny Black the use of h8 for his King.

All these last few examples have featured only minimal numbers of pieces on the board. They represent the area of technical endgames which can be analysed precisely to a win or draw. In general, of course, such positions would arise only after prolonged play in more complex, more obscure positions, with both sides striving to increase their advantages and fight back on parts of the board where they may stand worse. But even with many pieces on the board, some of the themes met in these simple positions may still be relevant. Before leaving Bishop-and-Knight endgames, let us see just one such finish from an international tournament game (Liberzon–Mititelu, Luhacovice 1971).

White to play in the diagram position on page 98 found an imaginative breach of Black's defences. With the Black King defending the Pawns on f6 and h6, and the Knight defending b7, all seems secure, but the defensive fortress was destroyed in just two moves:

1 b5! axb5 *2 Bxb7!* and after this surprising move Black resigned the game. *2 ...* Nxb7 allows *3 a6* and nothing can stop the Pawn from becoming a new Queen in two more moves. Equally, if Black does not take the Bishop at his second move, then White will still play his a-Pawn through to the queening square. One final variation before leaving this position: after *1 b5*, suppose Black had seen what was coming and ignored the Pawn with *1 ... Kh7*. Then White proceeds with *2 Bxb7!* anyway, since *2 Nxb7 3 bxa6* leads by another route to our familiar situation with Pawn on a6 winning against Knight on b7.

We have assumed in this and earlier cases that to be a Queen for a Knight ahead is indeed a decisive advantage. If many Pawns remain on the board, the win should be easy, with the Queen attacking undefended enemy Pawns and the Knight simply unable to cope with rapid changes of direction of attack. Even without Pawns, Queen beats Knight with little difficulty; the technique exhibits some instructive features.

White wins by a process of restriction and driving back:

1	Kd4	Nf5+
2	Kc5	Ne7
3	Qd6+	Kf7
4	Qd7	Kf6
5	Kd6	Nf5+
6	Kd5	Ne7+
7	Ke4	Ng6
8	Qf5+	Kg7
9	Qg5	Kf7
10	Kf5	Ne7+
11	Ke5	Ng6+
12	Kd6	Nf8

13 Qe7+ Kg8 14 Qe8 Kg7 15 Ke7 Ng6+ 16 Ke6 Nf8+
17 Kf5 Nh7 18 Qg6+ Kh8 19 Qf7 and White finally wins
the Knight. The last ditch try 19 ... Ng5 is met not by 20 Kxg5
stalemate, but by 20 Qe8+ and 21 Kxg5. Note how in this
endgame White is simply repeating a similar process again and
again. Compare the positions after 2 Kc5, 7 Ke4, 12 Kd6 and
17 Kf5. The formation of the pieces is exactly the same, each
time with the Black King nearer the corner of the board. Such a
process is quite typical for many endgames: a repetition of a
forcing-back procedure, each time reaching a similar position
but with the defending King restricted to an ever-decreasing
sector of the board.

Before returning to our main theme of this chapter, endgames
with pieces and pawns, let us dispose of some more of the
basic endgames with no pawns, but with pieces of both colours
on the board.

Firstly, we should mention that King and Rook does not
generally win against King and Knight. Replacing the Queen by
a Rook in the previous diagram, play might continue 1 Kd4
Nf5+ 2 Ke4 Nd6+ 3 Kd4 Nf5+ 4 Kc5 Ke5 5 Rf1 Ne3
6 Re1 Ke4 7 Kd6 Kd4, and White continues to make no
progress. Only when the King and Knight are widely separated,
or already confined to a corner of the board, should the Rook
stand much chance of forcing a win. King and Rook against
King and Bishop is also normally a draw. Even in an extreme
case, the defending side can just hang on to save the game as the
diagram on page 100 shows.

Though forced right to a corner, Black does not lose, thanks to
a stalemate resource. After 1 Rf8+ Bb8, either 2 Ka6 or any
horizontal Rook move gives a draw by stalemate. Therefore,
White must relax his bind. 2 Rf5 Bd6 3 Ra5+ Kb8 4 Rd5
Bc7+! 5 Kc6 Bg3, and Black preserves enough King room to
avoid being mated. It is important in this extreme position that
Black's King is in a corner of opposite colour square to his
Bishop. Move all the pieces one square to the right and White
wins by an elegant, though not difficult manoeuvre: 1 Rc7!
(stopping the King from fleeing to c8 at any time) 1 ... Be4+
2 Kb6 Bb1 (the Bishop hides from the Rook; 2 ... Bd3 3
Rd7 or 2 ... Bf5 3 Rf7 would lose more quickly) 3 Rc1 Be4
4 Re1 Bg6 5 Re6 Bh5 6 Rh6 Bg4 7 Rh8+ Bc8 8 Rg8
(not now stalemate) 8 ... Ka8 9 Rxc8 mate. The duel
between Rook and Bishop in this play is an easy win for the
heavier piece.

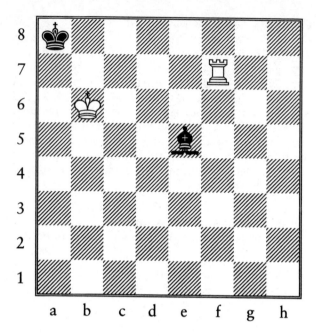

Another interesting tussle is that of Queen against Rook. This is generally a win for the Queen, but the process of forcing back the defending King can be long and arduous. The next diagram shows a possible late stage in the procedure. White rounds off his attack with 1 Qe8! Ra7 (1 ... Rb8 2 Qe7+ Kc8 3 Kc6 wins immediately for White) 2 Qe7+ Kb8 3 Qd8+ Kb7 4 Kb5 and Black must move his Rook with fatal results: 4 ... Ra8 5 Qd7+ Kb8 6 Kb6, or 4 ... Ra3 5 Qe7+, or 4 ... Ra2 5 Qd5+, or 4 ... Ra1 5 Qd5+ Kc8 (other moves lose the Rook to a check on e5 or d4) 6 Qg8+ Kd7 7 Qg7+. In all variations the Rook is finally lost to a forking check.

There is an amusing trap also embedded in this play: suppose after 1 Qe8 Ra7 2 Qe7+ Kb8 White continues less accurately with 3 Qd6+ Kc8, then already he must play with the utmost care. 4 Kb6?, powerful though it looks, allows a draw by 4 ... Ra6+! 5 Kxa6 is stalemate, other moves lose the Queen. Even the restrained 4 Kb5? would allow a surprising draw with 4 ... Rb7+ 5 Ka6 (5 Kc6 Rb6+! 6 Kxb6 stalemate) Ra7+! 6 Kb5 (taking the Rook is still stalemate) Rb7+ 7 Kc5 Rc7+ 8 Kb4 Rb7+ and the Black Rook checks on. If the King ever ventures to the d-file, the Queen will be lost to ... Rd7.

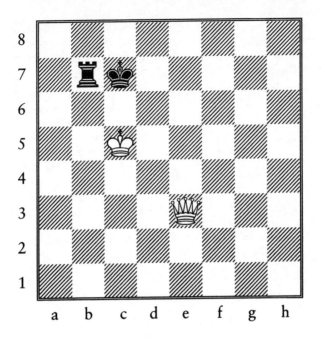

Rook- and Pawn-endgames

Of all pieces on the chessboard, the Rooks are best designed to
survive until the endgame. Starting the game walled in behind
Pawns, they have to await the opening of files before they can
join in the active play. There are usually plenty of opportunities
for Knights and Bishops to be exchanged off the board before
the Rooks come into their own. For this reason, Rook-and-
Pawn endgames are among the most commonly encountered on
the chessboard. Even apparently simple positions can contain a
wealth of subtlety; indeed a whole book could be written on the
theory of the positions with just Rook and Pawn against Rook.
In such a deceptively easy sounding endgame, the margin
between a win and a draw can be so narrow that even great
masters have been known to err in their judgments and their
play of such positions.

In endgames with a Rook and several Pawns each, some general
principles can be enunciated. Above all, it is important to try to
play actively with both Rook and King. The Rook should
ideally be attacking enemy Pawns rather than passively
defending one's own. The King should be supporting the attack,

and aiding the advance of any passed Pawns which can be created. The ability of the Rook to control whole ranks or files is particularly important in that it can create a barrier beyond which the enemy King cannot pass.

This position is a simple example of the strength of an active Rook. Playing *1 Rd7!* White confines the Black King to the back rank, and the Rook on b8 is tied to the defence of the b-Pawn. *1 . . . Ke8* would lose the g-Pawn, while *1 . . . b6 2 c6! Rc8 3 c7* leaves Black facing the threat of *4 Rd8+* which would ensure the coronation of the Pawn.

Finally, if Black chooses to sit tight with moves such as Kg8, Kf8, etc., then the White King will join the attack, playing either to e3, d4, d5, d6 and c7 to win the Q-side Pawns, or to g2, h3, h4 and g5, going after the Pawns on the other wing. After *1 Rd7*, White would indeed have every prospect of winning the game.

Let us now revert to some simpler positions, where some of the ideas of Rook-and-Pawn endgames can be seen in their purest form. First, a surprising position which dates back to an analysis by F. Saavedra in 1895. White to play wins, but only after some astonishing twists and turns (see diagram on page 103).

1 c7 Rd6+ (Black has no other move to prevent the Pawn from queening next move.)

2 Kb5! (*2 Kb7? Rd7!* gives a draw with Rxc7 next move. More subtlety, *2 Kc5?* is a mistake because of *2 . . . Rd1!* and *3 . . . Rc1+*. For this reason, White avoids the c-file with his King.)

2 . . . Rd5+ 3 Kb4! Rd4+ 4 Kb3 Rd3+ 5 Kc2! Rd4! A brilliant resource by Black. Now *6 c8=Q* is met by *6 . . . Rc4+! 7 Qxc4* stalemate! Yet White can still win.

6 c8=R!

An amazing position is reached in which King and Rook beats King and Rook. The stalemate trick no longer works; meanwhile White threatens to force mate with *7 Ra8*. Black has only one move.

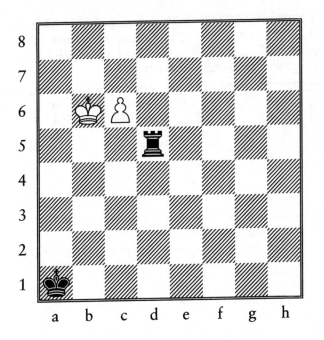

6 ... Ra4

But now comes *7 Kb3!* threatening both *8 Kxa4* and *8 Rc1* mate. Black must lose his Rook or be mated.

One of the amusing features of that position is that Black's elegant stalemate resource is based upon precisely the same circumstance as White's even more elegant refutation: the position of the Black King in the corner. If all the pieces were moved one file to the right, neither the stalemate nor the final mating idea would work at all.

That position, of course, was rather an exception to what one would normally expect in such a simple endgame, but the idea is too neat to leave without another related example. The next position, discovered by Selesniev, involves the White King in a similar exercise, running up and down the board to escape the attentions of a persistent Rook:

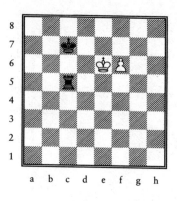

1 f7 Rc6+   2 Ke5!
(Not 2 Ke7? Rc1! 3 f8=Q
Re1+ 4 Kf7 Rf1+ winning the
Queen.)
2 ... Rc5+   3 Ke4!
(Always the White King avoids
the f-file. 3 Kf4? Rc1! would
even win for Black.)
3 ... Rc4+   4 Ke3 Rc3+
5 Kf2 Rc2+   6 Kg3 Rc3+
7 Kg4 Rc4+   8 Kg5 Rc5+
9 Kg6 Rc6+   10 Kg7!

Finally the King is safe from the Rook checks and the Pawn can
safely promote to a Queen next move. After 10 ... Rc1 11
f8=Q Rg1+ the White King approaches the Rook on g- and h-files
until the checks run out. Finally the Queen should win against the
lone Rook. It is worth noting that White does need the h-file to
escape the Rook's attentions. Move everything one file to the right
in the initial position and White can no longer win.

That last comment illustrates how difficult it can be to assess
endgame positions at a glance. What is important if one is to
acquire good endgame technique is not so much a perfect
memory for which positions are won and which drawn, but a
sound knowledge of the procedures needed to win or draw
them. The ability to work out precisely what is happening in a
position is far more useful than an extensive memory of
thousands of specific cases.

We conclude this chapter with a few more typical positions of
Rook and Pawn against Rook, which illustrate some of the most
commonly encountered ideas.

In the next position White to play wins; Black to play draws. If
it is White's move, he plays the neat 1 Rh8! either promoting
the Pawn or winning Black's Rook by an X-ray after 1 ...
Rxa7 2 Rh7+. Black to move, however, avoids this trick by
playing 1 ... Kg7! Any White Rook move just loses the Pawn,
and White's King cannot help: 2 Kf1 Ra1+ 3 Ke2 Ra2+
4 Kd3 Ra3+ 5 Kc4 Ra4+ 6 Kb5 Ra1 7 Kb6 Rb1+!
8 Kc6 Ra1 9 Kb7 Rb1+ 10 Kc6 Ra1 and the White King
cannot hide from the checks while defending the a-Pawn to free
his Rook.

Compare in that last example the relative freedom of Black's Rook, placed behind the passed Pawn, with White's Rook in front of it. It is often asserted as a general principle that Rooks belong behind passed Pawns. So placed, their activity increases with every advance of the Pawn. Like all other rules, it has exceptions, but it is a useful principle to remember nevertheless.

In general, Rook and Pawn against Rook does not win if the defending King can occupy a square in front of the Pawn. The defensive technique is illustrated by the diagram on page 106.

White to play can drive the King back with *1 Rh7+ Ke8*, but what is more important is that his own King cannot advance beyond the fifth rank. After *2 e6*, he would threaten *3 Kf6* and *4 Rh8* mate, but Black defends with *3 . . . Ra1! 4 Kf6 Rf1+ 5 Ke5 Re1+ 6 Kd6 Rd1+* and White's King must retreat from its threatening position. If instead White waits with *2 Rb7* instead of *2 e6*, Black can be patient too: *2 . . . Rc6 3 Ra7 Rb6*. Eventually White has nothing better than *4 e6*, when *4 . . . Rb1!* defends again. Note that *2 Rb7 Ra1?* would make Black's task far harder; *3 Kf6 Rf1+ 4 Ke6!* already threatens mate, and Black has no good check. He should have waited on the third rank with his Rook until the white Pawn occupied e6.

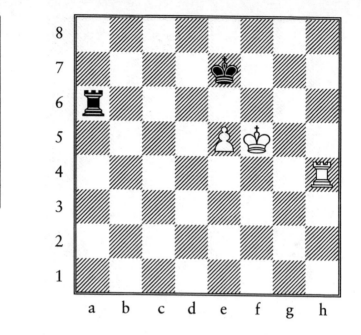

In order to win such an endgame of Rook and Pawn against Rook, White should try to support the passed Pawn with his King, while using his Rook to prevent the defending King from approaching. The next diagram illustrates the successful finish of such a procedure. It is a famous position, known by the name of Lucena, a fifteenth-century Spanish chess writer (though the position is not in fact to be found in his works).

White's King cannot move to free the way for his Pawn to advance. His Rook must be used both to drive away the Black King and to provide an eventual shelter for White's King. The winning procedure is very instructive: **1 Re1+ Kd7 2 Re4!** (a very important move: 2 Kf7 Rf2+ 3 Kg6 Rg2+ 4 Kf6 Rf2+ 5 Ke5 Rg2 gets White nowhere) **2 . . . Rh1** (2 . . . Rf2 would lose quickly to 3 Rh4 and 4 Kh8) **3 Kf7 Rf1+ 4 Kg6 Rg1+ 5 Kf6 Rf1+ 6 Kg5 Rg1+ 7 Rg4!** Finally the reason becomes clear for playing 2 Re4. The Rook shelters the King and ensures the promotion of the Pawn. But let us go back a couple of moves; suppose instead of 5 . . . Rf1+ Black had played simply 5 . . . Rg2. Then White builds his shelter further up the board: 6 Re5 with Rg5 to follow again secures the desired objective. At the very least, Black must surrender his Rook for the Pawn.

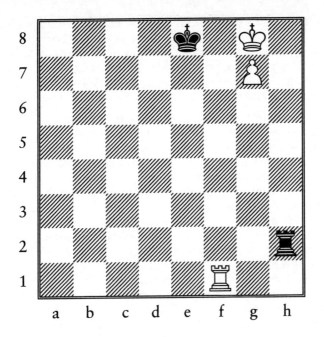

With the Lucena position, we come to the end of this short introduction to endgame technique. It is no more possible to summarisze the rules of good endgame play than it is possible to provide a clear set of instructions for playing good chess, but there are certain principles which do emerge from the study of positions such as we have seen in this chapter.

1 If you have a majority of Pawns on one side of the board, advance them correctly and try to create a passed Pawn. The value of a passed Pawn lies as much in its ability to distract enemy pieces from other defensive duties as in its threats to advance and become a Queen. A single passed Pawn is often insufficient to win by its own efforts, but enough to force an entry on the other side of the board.

2 Keep your pieces, including your King, as active as possible, attacking the enemy Pawns rather than passively defending. In the endgame the King can have the attacking potential approximately equal to that of a Knight or Bishop.

3 When very few Pawns remain on the board, a single Pawn advantage is often insufficient to win. Even with two extra Pawns, never assume that the game is going to win itself.

4 If you are a Pawn ahead, try to exchange the other pieces, keeping as many Pawns as possible on the board. Since a King- and Pawn-endgame with an extra Pawn is usually a win, every exchange of heavier pieces brings the win closer. Equally, if defending an endgame a Pawn behind, try to exchange Pawns, keeping the other men on the board.

In the endgame more than in any other phase of the game, patience and precision are all-important. A hasty move can turn a win into a draw, a draw into a loss or even a win into a loss. As the number of pieces on the board is reduced, the cut and thrust of tactical threats becomes less important. The players have moved out of a world of sudden attacks and hazardous adventures into an area where there begins to be room for certainty instead of hope, and precise evaluation of the possibilities in place of a more fumbling, groping thought process. The endgame is the realm of pure chess logic. Every chessplayer gradually builds up his own knowledge of positions that are won, drawn or lost. Every game must eventually find its way into one of these types of position. Until then, they hover around the uncertain areas of advantage and disadvantage. The art of good endgame play is a sure technique to handle the textbook won and drawn positions, combined with the skill to recognize when an advantageous position may be turned into a definite win. Above all, what marks the strong players from weaker ones is the ability and the perseverance to defend disadvantageous endgame positions, without letting them be pushed over the edge into the hopelessness of the technical loss.

Further examples and exercises

1 True endgame skill is a combination of knowledge, calculation and imagination. You may know certain standard endgames, but recognizing how to reach them, or their modified versions, is another matter entirely.

Try this one. It is Black to play and he is two Pawns down. How does he save himself, using one of the ideas we have just seen?

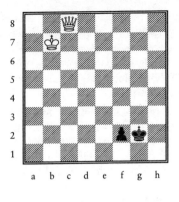

2 We have seen positions in which one side is a Bishop and a Pawn ahead yet cannot win; we have seen positions in which material is level, yet one side's game is hopeless. Here is another example of the apparent unfairness of some endgames: White is Queen for Pawn ahead, yet the game is a draw. After *1 Qg4+ Kh2 2 Qf3 Kg1 3 Qg3+* Black does not play *3 . . . Kf1?*, blocking his own Pawn and letting the white King approach, but *3 . . . Kh1!* when *4 Qxf2* is stalemate, while *4 Qf3+ Kg1* or *4 Qf4 Kg2* fails to make any progress. This stalemate trick only works with the f-Pawn or c-Pawn. A Queen will generally win against e-Pawn or d-Pawn on the seventh rank, though a-Pawn or h-Pawn draw for a different reason. See if you can work out what happens if the black Pawn is on h2 instead of f2.

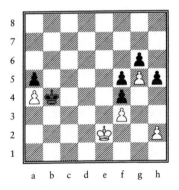

3 White to play and you are about to lose your a-Pawn. You may dream of saving the game with *1 Kd3 Kxa4 2 Kc4*, but after *2 . . . h4 3 h3 Ka3 4 Kc3 a4 5 Kc2 Kb4 6 Kb2 Kc4*, Black wins with the usual ploy of dashing to the K-side while White wastes time capturing the a-Pawn. Yet White can draw the diagram position in no more than five moves. How does he do it?

Hint: think of all the ways a game can be drawn.

Answers

1 Black forces a draw with *1 . . .* Bh3! After *2* gxh3 White has doubled h-Pawns and a Bishop which does not control h8. Just as with a single Pawn, he has no way to expel the black king from h8. If White does not take the Bishop, Black plays *2 . . .* Bxg2, reaching the same standard drawn endgame.

2 With the black Pawn on h2 instead of f2 in the diagram, play may continue *1* Qg4+ Kh1 *2* Qf3+ Kg1 *3* Qg3+ Kh1 and the white Queen must move again since any King move is stalemate. So *4* Qh3 Kg1 *5* Qe3+ Kg2 *6* Qe2+ Kg1 *7* Qg4+ Kh1 and so on. There is no way for White to force the King to h1, other than b y setting up a potential stalemate that must immediately be lifted. The game is a draw.

3 White saves the game by the remarkable expedient of stalemating himself: *1* Kf2! Kxa4 *2* Kg2 Kb3 *3* Kh3 a4 *4* Kh4 a3 *5* h3 a2 stalemate. Other Black plans also fail to prevent White's self-incarceration. For example *1* Kf2 h4 *2* Kg2 h3+ *3* Kxh3 and again *4* Kh4 and *5* h3 forces stalemate. Or *1* Kf2 Kc3 *2* Kg2 Kd3 *3* Kh3 Ke3 *4* Kh4 Kxf3 *5* h3 and whatever Black does it is again stalemate.

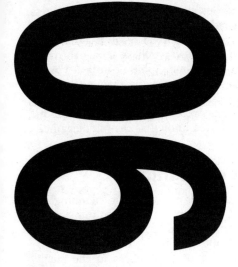

06

strategic planning

In this chapter you will learn:
- the elements of positional play: material, space and initiative, and how they each contribute to an overall judgement of the position
- how to identify weaknesses in your opponent's position and how to take advantage of them.

As we have seen in the previous chapter, the endgame in chess can be a precisely conducted stage of the game, where the players' intentions are clear and the correct result is a matter of concrete analysis. Equally, since every chess game starts in precisely the same position, the opening phase can be a voyage across well-charted waters. But *between* the opening and the endgame, when both sides have developed their armies but numbers are not reduced to a state where endgame technique can take over, comes the vast area known as the middlegame.

The assessment of positions

The key to good middlegame play is strategic planning, by which we mean the art of deciding what to do and how to improve one's position when no clear gains are available by brutal tactical means. Good chess is characterized by systematically taking advantage of weaknesses in the enemy position, while avoiding serious defects in one's own. In this chapter we shall be discussing the nature of such weaknesses: how to recognize them, how to exploit them, how to create them where it may seem none exists. The good chessplayer is always asking the questions: how can I make my own position better, how can I make my opponent's game worse? Where are the weak points in his position and how can I exploit them? What are the strong points in my position, how can I increase them? The very best chess games are not brief battles decided by a single bloody skirmish, but masterpieces of delicate manoeuvring, with one side gradually building up his advantage until the enemy succumbs.

Material, space and the initiative

When one begins to play chess, the middlegame appears as a minefield of tactical traps. The objectives of play seem primarily to win the opponent's pieces, to deliver short, sharp, decisive attacks, and to avoid making crass errors. Experience takes us beyond this elementary stage to a level where more subtle considerations begin to assume a pre-eminent role. As we play more, our judgement of positions becomes ever more refined. In this chapter we shall introduce some of the concepts which are important in the formation of positional judgements. If there are no immediate tactical resources for either player, overall assessment of a position must depend on three main factors:

1 **Material** The basic question of who has more pieces, or to be more precise, pieces of higher value, is the first thing one looks at in arriving at an assessment of a position. In general, to win a game with an extra Knight, Bishop, Rook or Queen, should be a simple matter of coordinating one's men into the attack. The side with superior force can always attack with more pieces than are available for defence. The attack ought therefore to succeed, all else being equal.

2 **Space** The command of territory on the board is the next most important factor. In general, one conquers territory by a systematic advance of Pawns. Since no piece will willingly be exchanged for a Pawn, the men of higher value must retreat when attacked by Pawns. Each side's Pawn front represents the limit of the space he controls. As we shall see in more detail later, the Pawns are responsible for creating outposts from which the other pieces can operate with maximum effect.

3 **Initiative** The most nebulous of the three basic elements, the initiative is a measure of which player is better placed to dictate the course of play. To be able to create direct threats, to be able to force the opponent's replies, these are advantages which restrict the opponent's freedom and may consequently lead to more substantial gains. Although the initiative may often appear to be synonymous with attack, it is also possible to hold the initiative when apparently on the defensive. Consolidating one's defences prior to driving back the attacking pieces can be as much a way of seizing control of the game as a more blatantly aggressive strategy.

Of these three components of positional assessment, the initiative is the most difficult to understand and the easiest to misjudge. Sometimes an apparently strong attack can fizzle out after a few moves, but equally an apparently small initiative, which starts as a mere annoyance, can steadily grow to assume the proportions of a winning advantage. Only experience helps us learn to assess whether an initiative will be enduring or not.

Pawn weaknesses and other positional factors

Before proceeding to discuss some examples of middlegame planning, we need to introduce a number of concepts from positional chess. The descriptions of Pawn structures, in particular, gives us a handy vocabulary for discussing the potential of a position and for identifying the correct strategies for the players. We have already met the Passed Pawn (one with no opposite number on its own or adjacent files in front to impede its progress to the queening square) and the Doubled Pawn (two Pawns of the same colour on the same file); we must now define some other useful varieties of Pawn.

Isolated Pawn: An isolated Pawn is a Pawn which has no Pawn of the same colour standing on an adjacent file. The isolated Pawn can thus never be defended by another Pawn unless a subsequent capture causes a Pawn to change file.

If two Pawns of the same colour stand on the same file, with no friendly Pawn on a neighbouring file, they are known as *doubled, isolated Pawns*. (For example, after the opening moves 1 e4 Na6 2 Bxa6 bxa6 Black already has doubled, isolated Pawns on the a-file.)

Backward Pawn: When a Pawn has fallen behind its colleagues, remaining on a modest rank while those to either side have rushed ahead, it is known as a backward Pawn. Strictly speaking, this term is generally reserved for a Pawn which has little or no immediate prospect of advancing to catch up the other Pawns. Like the isolated Pawn, the backward Pawn is unable to be defended by another Pawn.

As we shall see from the examples which follow, backward and isolated Pawns have implications for a position which may extend far beyond the strength or weakness of the Pawn itself.

The Pawns on a3, g5 and g4 in the next diagram are isolated Pawns. Those on d2 and f2 are backward Pawns. The creation of backward Pawns carries the potentially serious side-effect of squares in one's own camp that invite an enemy invasion. In this position, the squares d3 and f3 in White's half of the board can never be controlled by White Pawns; consequently any Black pieces which find their way to d3 or f3 cannot be expelled by attack from a Pawn. Such squares are known as *weak squares*, or *holes*, and form a natural object of attention for enemy forces looking for an outpost.

The black Pawn on c7 has some symptoms of backwardness, which can be cured by its advance to c6. (Note that its advance to c5 would leave the Pawns on b6 and d6 backward.) If White, however, were to establish a piece on c6, then the c7-Pawn would remain backward.

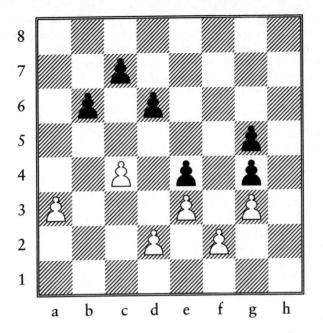

The weakness of the backward Pawn is twofold: if it stays behind, it is liable to become immobilized and an object of attack, but just as important its very existence implies the presence of a hole which can be occupied by enemy pieces, with no fear of being kicked away.

Returning to the same diagram, there are two other positional features connected with the Pawn formations which can usefully be defined at this point:

An *open file* is any file which has no Pawns on it.

A *half-open file* is a file which has on it only a Pawn or Pawns of one colour.

Thus in the diagram position, the h-file is the only open file, but the a-, b- and f-files are all half-open. Naturally enough, open files are the ideal domain for Rooks, which need the wide open spaces in order to operate freely. An isolated or backward Pawn on a half-open file can also be an attraction for the attention of a Rook. Black Rooks on the f- or a-files in the diagram position would be attacking the White Pawns on those files and would consequently tie down White pieces to their defence.

One final comment before we leave the topic of pure Pawn formations: in general, the zig-zag Pawn structure (such as the White Pawns on d2, e3, f2, g3 in the diagram) is generally inadvisable. With all the Pawns on squares of the same colour, a whole collection of weaknesses is created on the other colour of square. This weakness can be mitigated by the possession of a Bishop to control the complementary squares. Such a Bishop, operating on squares of opposite colour to those upon which its own Pawns stand, is often termed a *good Bishop*. The *bad Bishop*, on the other hand, is one which is hampered by its own Pawns and does not control those squares which the Pawns neglect.

As both sides' Pawns advance in their attempts to gain territory, the Pawn fronts can easily become locked together, with one side's Pawns predominately on white squares, the other's on black. We then talk about a player being 'strong on the black squares', or 'having white square weaknesses'. Once the colour-complex has been identified, the importance of good and bad Bishops can become one of the most important positional considerations. A white-squared Bishop aided only by white-squared Pawns can leave half the board effectively uncontrollable, and be an invitation for the enemy pieces to invade on the black squares.

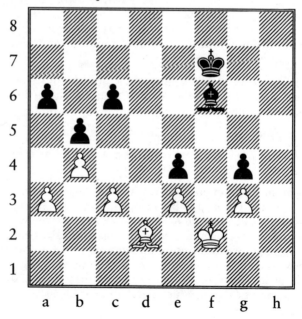

A characteristic example of good Bishop versus bad Bishop. Black has every chance of victory by organizing a concerted attack on the White Pawns with King and Bishop: **1 . . . Ke6 2 Ke2 Kd5 3 Kd1 Kc4 4 Kc2** (White reaches this square just in time to defend his c-Pawn) **4 . . . Be5 5 Be1 Bc7 6 Bf2 Bd6 7 Be1 Be5**. White is in the unhappy situation known as *zugzwang* – a compulsion to move when one would prefer to pass. Any White move will lose something: if the Bishop moves, either g-Pawn or c-Pawn is lost; **8 Kd2** loses the c-Pawn, while **8 Kb2** allows decisive infiltration with **8 . . . Kd3**, winning the K-side Pawns quickly. Black's advantage should be enough to win comfortably.

We have deliberately chosen an endgame position to illustrate this theme because it is most clear when the board is uncluttered by other pieces. But even with other men on the board, White would stand at a considerable disadvantage, having a Bishop hampered by its own Pawns and, even more important, no satisfactory defence to a white-square invasion threat.

Interestingly, the starting position is no better for White even if his Bishop stands on d4. Black wins with **1 . . . Bd8!** (keeping the advantage by maintaining the presence of Bishops on the board) **2 Ke2 Bc7 3 Kf2 Ke6**, with Kd5, Kc4, Kb3 and Kxa3 to follow.

Black would then finish off the game with a5 and the creation of a decisive passed Pawn on the Q-side. Alternatively, if White tries to prevent the deployment of the Black Bishop on the h2–b8 diagonal with **2 Be5**, then he is faced with an impossible choice after **2 . . . Ke6**. The Bishop cannot stay on both important diagonals. **3 Bf4** loses the c-Pawn to **3 . . . Bf6**, while **3 Bd4 Bc7** again ties the White King to the defence of g3, leaving the Black King free to create havoc on the other side of the board.

The subject of good and bad Bishops brings us to the question of the relative value of Bishop and Knight. In general it may be said that a Knight is better than a bad Bishop, but worse than a good one. Bishops need open lines to operate freely, so the more the Pawns are blocked against one another, obstructing the diagonals, the worse Bishops become. The diagram below is a position composed by A. Troitsky, which could well have occurred in a game. It is a surprising illustration of the manner in which even a single Pawn on its own colour of square can be fatal for a Bishop.

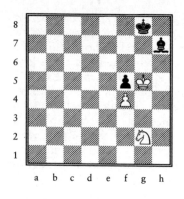

White wins with

1 Kh6 Kh8
2 Nh4 Kg8
3 Nf3 Kh8
4 Ne5 Kg8
5 Nc6 Kh8
6 Ne7 Bg8
7 Ng6 mate

Black has no option at any stage, since other moves lead always to immediate loss of the Bishop or mate by Ng6.

Two further points to note about this position: firstly, that 1 Nh4 Kg7 2 Nxf5 Bxf5 3 Kxf5 Kf7 is only a draw; but, more importantly, that without the Pawn on f5, Black would draw the game with great ease. His Bishop stands guard on the b1–h7 diagonal and gives its life for the f-Pawn as soon as it dares advance.

This has all strayed some way from the theme of middlegames, so, with the concept of good and bad Bishops now clearly established, let us return to more complex positions.

The formulation and execution of a strategic plan

The first example is taken from a game Marshall–Burn played in Paris in 1900. Both sides have practically completed the development of their pieces. It is White's move and he is ready to determine his plan for the middlegame. The features of the position which one should notice are the half-open c- and e-files, the potentially backward Black c-Pawn and the fact that Black has a Bishop whereas White has a Knight. Neither of Black's Bishops at the moment is particularly effective. His white-squared Bishop is blocked by the Pawn on d5, while the other Bishop is just as effectively limited by White's well-supported Pawn on d4. This consideration, together with the backwardness of the c-Pawn, should suggest the correct plan for Black: to advance his Pawn to c5 and try to exchange the White d-Pawn, thereby enhancing the scope of the Black Bishops. If we imagine the moves . . . c5, dxc5 and . . . bxc5 played from the diagram position, we see that both Bishops have suddenly come to life. One has a much freer diagonal from f6, while the other is ready to burst into action by an advance of the Black d-Pawn.

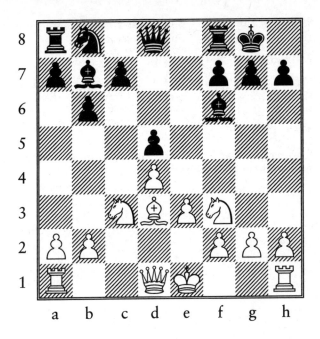

But as we said, it is White's move. He naturally wants to keep the central position closed. Marshall was a gifted American player noted for his devastating attacks. In this game, he saw a line of attack along the diagonal b1–h7. White might consider playing Bc2 followed by Qd3 to threaten Qh7 mate, but Marshall found a more enduring way to continue:

1 h4!

He sees that the Rook on h1 can effectively join the attack. Very often a Pawn advance such as this can result in the opening of lines for the Rooks. The Pawn on h4 is also designed to support an advance of the Knight to g5 to join the attack on h7.

1 ... g6

Black decides to close the diagonal to h7.

2 h5 Re8   3 hxg6 hxg6

Without even moving, the Rook on h1 is already part of the attack. Now White needs to find a way for his Queen to join it.

4 Qc2 Nd7

Perhaps Black thought that Qc2 was a harmless preparation for castling Q-side. The real point is now revealed.

5 Bxg6! fxg6   6 Qxg6+ Bg7   7 Ng5

White has given up a Bishop for two Pawns, but the Black King is completely exposed to attack. The immediate threat is 8 Qf7 mate.

7 . . . Qf6

Defending against the mate on f7, but allowing a neat combinational finish instead.

8 Rh8+! Kxh8   9 Qh7 mate

White's play is admirable for its purposefulness, even single-mindedness. The opening of the h-file, the destruction of the shelter round the enemy King, and the final onrush of pieces for the mating attack were all accomplished with the utmost economy. Black's own counter-attacking plans never even had the chance to get started.

The following position is another example of a devastating attack as the consequence of a logical, aggressive plan when only just out of the opening.

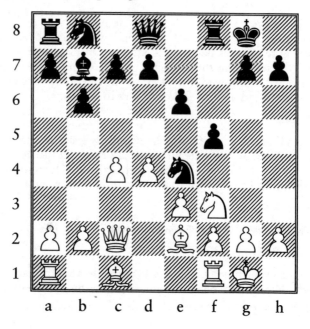

Black to move, from a game Litvinov–Veresov, Minsk 1958. Black sees the attacking potential of his Bishop against the Pawn on g2. Reasoning that White would like to drive the menacing Knight away from e4, Black builds up his attack on the K-side, in expectation of the White Knight's retreat from f3.

1 . . . Rf6

The Rook heads for g6 or h6 to bear down on the Pawns sheltering White's King.

2 Nd2 Rh6

Without an open file along which to operate, the Rook has shifted in front of its own Pawns to achieve a similar activity. Already Black should be envisaging a continuation such as 3 Nxe4 Bxe4   4 Qd1 Qh4   5 h3 Bxg2!   6 Kxg2 Qxh3+   7 Kg1 Qh1 mate.

3 g3

White wants to guard against . . . Qh4 as well as removing his Pawn from the attention of the Bishop. Laudable motives, but he has overlooked something remarkable.

3 . . . Qh4!

Black plays this move all the same. If White takes the Queen he is mated: 4 gxh4 Rg6+   5 Kh1 Nxf2 is double check and mate.

4 Nf3 Ng5!

The final point to Black's winning combination.

The following variations are worth playing through to appreciate the brilliance of the whole conception:

(a) 5 Nxh4 Nh3 is mate
(b) 5 gxh4 Nxf3+   6 Kg2 (or 6 Kh1) Nxd4+ and 7 . . . Nxc2 leaves Black a piece ahead
(c) 5 gxh4 Nxf3+   6 Bxf3 Rg6+   7 Bg2 (7 Kh1 Bxf3 is mate) 7 . . . Rxg2+   8 Kh1 Rxf2+   9 Kg1 Rxc2 and again Black is decisively ahead on material.

What is important here is not the flashiness of the final combination, beautiful though it is, but the logical way it stemmed from Black's attacking plan. When he played 1 . . . Rf6, Black had only vague thoughts of shifting the Rook sideways. He had no means of knowing that White's Knight would, in fact, willingly retreat from f3 (in fact, White's 2 Nd2 is a very bad error of judgment), but felt that the Black Rook would be ready to attack from g6 or h6 if convenient. Under other circumstances, Black might even have found himself thinking about playing . . . g5 and g4 to expel the Knight from f3. White's cooperative play just made the plan all the more effective.

In both this example and the previous one we should stress the difference between the plan itself and the individual moves played in the realization of that plan. Strategic planning in chess can stem from an imprecise, fuzzy sort of thought process. In the Marshall–Burn position, White's plan may be expressed as follows: to induce Black to play . . . g6 by creating a threat on the b1–h7 diagonal, to advance the white h-Pawn to open a line for the Rook, and finally to demolish Black's defences with a sacrifice on g6. By playing 1 h4, rather than 1 Qc2 or 1 Bc2, White commits himself to attack but keeps open his options as to where his Queen will develop. The move 1 h4 is based upon a more detailed analysis of the precise probable continuations than was necessary for the mere formulation of the plan. Yet without the formulation of that plan in the first place, the move 1 h4 would never have suggested itself.

Similarly, in the Litvinov–Veresov game, the move 1 . . . Rf6 is based upon a realization of the attacking potential of Queen and Rook both on the h-file, particularly in conjunction with the Bishop operating from long distance at b7. Of course, it takes some imagination to conceive of the attacking idea, particularly when the White Knight is still on f3, but any aggressively minded player keen to get at his opponent's King would have little difficulty in formulating this plan.

Let us proceed to a longer, and far more positional example.

The position opposite occurred after fifteen moves on each side of the game Alekhine–Yates, London 1922. White has the advantage thanks to two important factors: his uncontested occupation of the only open file on the board and Black's problem Bishop which cannot control the black squares already weakened by his saw-tooth Pawn formation in the centre. Alekhine, who was later to become the World Champion, proved that these advantages were enough to win the game. Play continued as follows:

16 Nb3 a4   17 Nc5 Nxc5   18 Qxc5! Qxc5
19 Rxc5 b4

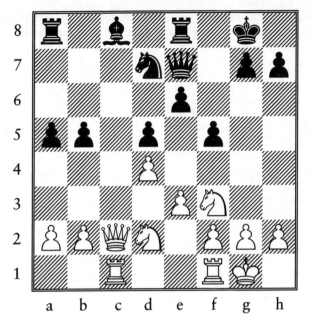

By exchanging Knights and Queens, White has accentuated his advantages. His Knight can now dominate the board from e5, while the other Rook is ready to come from f1 to join its colleague on the open file. Note that the recapture with the Pawn on c5 on either of White's last two moves would have been inferior since it would have diminished White's control of the e5 square, allowing Black's Pawn to advance and remedy his black-square weakness. Also, the resulting White Pawn on c5 would have blocked the open file, lessening the effect of White's Rooks.

20 Rfc1 Ba6 21 Ne5 Reb8

It should be noticed that Black cannot contest the open file with 21 . . . Rec8 since 22 Rxc8+ Rxc8 23 Rxc8+ Bxc8 24 Nc6, by threatening both Nxb4 and Ne7+, would win at least a Pawn. Now White's pieces are all beautifully placed, but his attack lacks the finishing touch. The winning strategy decided upon involves bringing the King into the attack.

**22 f3 b3   23 a3 h6   24 Kf2 Kh7   25 h4 Rf8
23 Kg3 Rfb8   27 Rc7 Bb5   28 R1c5 Ba6   29 R5c6 Re8
30 Kf4 Kg8   31 h5 Bf1   32 g3 Ba6**

The stage is set for the final invasion. The next part of the plan involves bringing both Rooks to the seventh rank to attack the g-Pawn.

33 Rf7 Kh7   34 R6c7 Rg8   35 Nd7 Kh8   36 Nf6!
(see diagram)

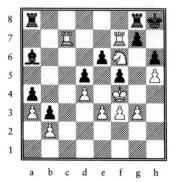

The Knight cannot be taken because of immediate mate on h7.

36 ...   Rgf8
37 Rxg7! Rxf6
38 Ke5!

A piquant finish. The Rook cannot be saved. *38 ... R* (either) f8 would be mated in two moves by *39 Rh7+ Kg8 40 Rcg7* mate.

Black resigned.

It is interesting to compare the positions in the two diagrams of that game. The essential feature of the position is preserved despite the passage of twenty moves: the White Pawns on d4 and e3, guarding the central black squares and leaving Black's rigid formation d5, e6, f5 unable to resist a gradual infiltration via the vacant e5 square. White's use of the open file is also very instructive: first dominating it with his Rooks, then using its occupation to enable a quick switch to the seventh rank and the decisive attack.

The role of planning in chess is frequently misunderstood. White did not, in that example, have 'a plan' which he carried out ruthlessly until it ended in mate. The plan is not such a guaranteed recipe for success, rather a series of sub-goals, each a step forward in the improvement of one's position. The occupation of the open file, bringing the King into the game, tying down the Black Rooks to defence of the e6-Pawn, these are all elements of a grand strategic design which need never be formulated in its entirety. A good strategic game often seems to be a series of small improvements, gradually increasing the pressure on the opponent's position until eventually something is bound to give way.

Chess strategy can hardly be learned the way openings and technical endgames can be memorized by rote. The game is too diverse even for a classification of strategic themes to be successfully accomplished. The best lessons in strategy are the games of the great masters. Anyone wishing to improve his own game should be encouraged to play through as many master games as he can get his hands on. At first, they will seem bewilderingly complex, but after a time, one begins to recognize ideas recurring time and again. Certain similarities of position are perceived which lead to the same type of play; pieces head for the same squares, Pawns are advanced in similar manners. And once these patterns are recognized, one can begin to incorporate their salient features into one's own games. The chapter of illustrative games in this book contains more wealth of strategic knowledge than can possibly be expressed in any formalized manner.

Before leaving this subject, however, let us look at just one last example, chosen to redress the balance after too many positions in which Knights proved superior to Bishops. Here is a game in which the Bishops proved too much for the cavalry.

The position overleaf was reached after White's 17th move of the game English–Steinitz, London 1863. There seems to be nothing that Black can attack in the White position. His Rooks cannot occupy aggressive posts on their open files, even the symmetrical nature of the Pawn formation prevents the formation of a passed Pawn. Yet Steinitz evolved a plan of gradual space-gaining by advancing his Pawns supported by the Bishops. This plan led to total success. From the very first move, he limits the action of the White Knight, until finally it cannot move at all.

1 ... b6   *2* h3 Be6   *3* Rfd1 c5   *4* Bg5 f6   *5* Bf4 Kf7

The first sign that the Bishops might be better than Bishop and Knight. Black can afford to bring his King closer to the action while White's must remain tucked behind its Pawns. If White plays Kf1, he is met by Bc4+, and must scurry back into safety. Note how Black willingly blocks the line of his own Bishop with f6, confident that this Pawn will be able to advance to f5 later.

6 f3 g5   *7* Rxd8 Rxd8   *8* Be3 h6

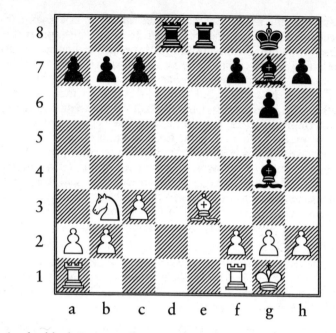

As the black Pawns advance, White has less and less room for his pieces. This last move gives added protection to the g-Pawn to enable f5 to be played.

9 Re1 f5   10 f4

White too can fight for space.

10 ... Bf6   11 g3 a5!

The last Pawn joins in the fight, adding its influence to force the retreat of the White Knight. White is powerless to counter this advance; his a-Pawn cannot advance without losing the Knight. It is important to note that 11 ... c4? would have been a bad error for Black, driving the Knight forward to d4, rather than back. With White's Knight or Bishop then firmly anchored on a fine central square, Black would have lost all his advantage. When gaining space progressively in this manner, it is important to ensure that one does not return ground already conquered. Black's threat is now to advance the a-Pawn to a4, then a3, undermining the Pawn on b2 which defends its colleague on c3.

12 Nc1 a4   13 a3 Bc4!

White has put a stop to the Q-side advance, but a primary objective has already been attained by Black. Note how the Bishop on c4 dominates the Knight. The Bishop controls every square the Knight might go to.

14 Kf2 gxf4   15 Bxf4 Bg5!

If White's Bishop is exchanged, the Black Rook will threaten to invade on d2.

16 Bxg5 hxg5   17 Ke3 Kf6   18 h4

White is running out of moves. *18 Ne2* would have been met by *18 . . . Rd3+   19 Kf2 Rd2* and the Q-side Pawns fall. We shall continue the game until its end, because the King and Pawn endgame is highly instructive.

18 . . . gxh4   19 gxh4 Re8+   20 Kf2 Rxe1
21 Kxe1 Ke5   22 Ne2 Bxe2   23 Kxe2 Kf4

In making these exchanges, Black had to calculate with great precision. He wins because of his well-placed King and because White's h-Pawn cannot be defended.

24 c4 Kg4   25 Ke3 f4+!   26 Ke4 f3   27 Ke3 Kg3
White resigned.

The Black Pawn will become a Queen (*28 h5 f2   29 Ke2 Kg2!*) and White's own passed Pawn is too far behind to put up any fight.

07

basic opening theory

In this chapter you will learn:
- the names of some of the most important chess openings and the ideas behind them
- examples of how the early moves may define the battle-lines for the rest of the game.

In Chapter 04, we discussed some of the principles which should be kept in mind while bringing out one's pieces at the start of a game. Since the chessmen begin each game on the same squares, it is reasonable that any game will, for a few moves at least, follow precisely the same course as other, earlier games. As succeeding generations of chessplayers have the opportunity to test new opening ideas in serious play, so we come to learn a great deal about the precise merits of certain moves in the early stages of a game. Some opening variations have been subjected to such intense scrutiny and practical tests that games may follow well-trodden paths for twenty or more moves on each side before one of the players chooses to diverge from previous practice.

Nevertheless, good opening play is not just a matter of remembering countless variations. Each separate opening should be looked upon as a plan for the development of the pieces. Within the broad framework of that plan, there is always room for flexibility, for innovation and improvization. Understanding the ideas behind each opening is far more important than keeping up with the latest developments of chess theory (though at a high level of play the strongest players find that it is almost a full-time task studying the games of their rivals to be sure that their latest ideas are understood).

In this chapter, we shall look at the essential ideas of some of the chess openings. In some cases, we shall pursue the analysis in more detail, if only to give a flavour of the type of results one can obtain by diligent research. Let us begin with an overview of the openings; there is a convenient classification, according to the opening move on each side.

Open games, beginning *1* e4 e5
Semi-open games, beginning *1* e4, Black not replying *1* . . . e5
Closed games, beginning *1* d4 d5
Semi-closed games, beginning *1* d4, Black not replying *1* . . . d5
Flank openings, beginning with any move other than *1* e4 or *1* d4

Most players, when starting to play chess, like to attack their opponents as quickly as possible. They therefore begin by playing *1* e4 in all their games, trying to develop their pieces as quickly as possible and create threats against the enemy King. As subtlety and sophistication creep gradually into one's chess understanding, however, one becomes more inclined to give more thought to proper preparation for attacks. In general, the openings with *1* e4 reach their crises earlier than *1* d4 openings or flank openings. As a player learns patience, and ceases to expect the decisive battles early in the game, he becomes more likely to change from *1* e4 openings to *1* d4. It should be said, however, that whatever the choice of first move, there is sufficient choice early in the game to allow enough freedom for the attacking or the cautious player to attempt to assert his style on the type of position which arises. We shall, in this chapter, concentrate our attention largely on the open games, an understanding of which is almost essential to any player's development.

Open games

The Giuoco Piano

Italian for 'Quiet Game', the Giuoco Piano is one of the oldest chess openings to have been analysed in depth. It is characterized by the moves *1* e4 e5 *2* Nf3 Nc6 *3* Bc4 Bc5. Both sides have brought out a Knight and a Bishop, the Bishops bear down on the vulnerable f-Pawns, and White is ready to castle. The most exciting play can follow if White now continues with *4* c3 (see diagram opposite). White prepares to form a big centre of Pawns with *5* d4, which would also gain time by attacking the Black Bishop. Note too that *4* c3 opens a diagonal for the Queen and introduces possibilities of Qb3 adding to the attack on f7.

Let us continue with the main line of analysis:

> *4* . . . Nf6

Black brings out another piece, attacks the e-Pawn and prepares to castle. Note that now *5* Ng5 would get White nowhere since *5* . . . 0-0 defends the f-Pawn adequately. 6 Qb3 would then be met by 6 . . . Qe7, leaving Black ready to drive back the attacking pieces with . . . h6 and . . . Na5, while instead of 6 Qb3, exchanging with 6 Nxf7 Rxf7 7 Bxf7+ Kxf7 would leave White with no pieces in play. Such an exchange early in the game of Bishop and Knight for Rook and Pawn is rarely advisable. White's Rooks remain ineffective until lines are open for them, while Black's Bishop and Knight already in play will ensure that he retains a useful initiative. So White continues with his planned central advance.

> *5* d4 exd4
> 6 cxd4 Bb4+!

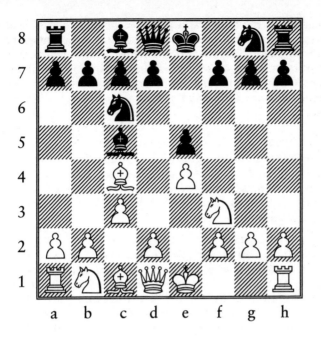

Meekly retreating with 6 ... Bb6 lets White push forward with 7 d5 perhaps even following by e5, chasing the Black Knights while gaining more and more space. By giving check with the Bishop, Black continues the fight for the initiative.

7 Nc3

White could avoid the ensuing complications with 7 Bd2, when 7 ... Bxd2+ 8 Nbxd2 d5! 9 exd5 Nxd5 is said to lead to a more or less equal game. A little trick worth noting here is that after 7 Bd2, if Black takes the e-Pawn, White easily regains the material: 7 ... Nxe4 8 Bxb4 Nxb4 9 Bxf7+! Kxf7 10 Qb3+ winning the Knight on b4.

7 ... Nxe4

Black accepts the offered Pawn; if he does not do so, he has nothing to show for White's central domination.

8 0-0

White's whole play is based on rapid development. By castling, he breaks the pin on his Knight, so is now threatening to capture on e4. But now he is offering a second Pawn on c3. With Black's

King still in the centre and the e-file open, White is ready to launch an immediate attack, but Black has little option but to grab the bait. There are two possibilities, according to whether Black captures on c3 with his Knight or Bishop. We shall look at the Knight capture first, but return later to see the possibilities stemming from 8 . . . Bxc3.

> 8 . . . Nxc3
> 9 bxc3 Bxc3

Black is now two Pawns ahead and is threatening the Rook on a1. He is ready to castle, and does not seem to be in any immediate danger, yet the White attack now turns out to be practically overwhelming; in fact he has a choice of attractive continuations:

(a) 10 Qb3 attacks the Bishop and supports the attack on f7. After 10 . . . Bxa1 11 Bxf7+ Kf8 (11 . . . Ke7 12 Bg5+ would lose the Queen) 12 Bg5 Ne7 13 Ne5, Black cannot withstand the combined onslaught of so many pieces. For example, 13 . . . Bxd4 14 Bg6 (threatening 15 Qf7 mate) 14 . . . d5 15 Qf3+ Bf5 16 Bxf5 Bxe5 17 Be6+ Bf6 18 Bxf6 gxf6 19 Qxf6+ Ke8 20 Qf7 mate. Yet after 10 Qb3, it is not too late for Black to bale out; he should play 10 . . . d5! 11 Bxd5 0-0! when 12 Qxc3 is met by 12 . . . Qxd5, while 12 Bxc6 is answered by 12 . . . Bxa1.

(b) Even stronger than 10 Qb3 is the apparently less forceful 10 Ba3! (see diagram opposite).

This quiet move ensures that the Black King remains trapped in the centre (he cannot castle through check). Even though Black may win a Rook, the White attack proves devastating. Since neither Black Rook can join in the game, White is effectively playing with a Rook more.

Let us look at some examples of how play might proceed:

(a) 10 . . . Bxa1 is immediately fatal for Black since 11 Re1+ Ne7 12 Bxe7 wins the Queen for insufficient material.

(b) 10 . . . d5 is a sensible try, hoping to shut one Bishop out of the attack. But White can change his attention to another diagonal: 11 Bb5 Bxa1 12 Re1+ Be6 13 Qa4! White threatens 14 Bxc6+, or even first to increase the pressure with 14 Ne5 (which move is particularly effective after 13 . . . Qd7). Even the desperate 14 . . . Kd7 15 Bxc6+ bxc6 16 Ne5+ Kc8 leads to mate after 17 Qa6+ Kb8 18 Nxc6.

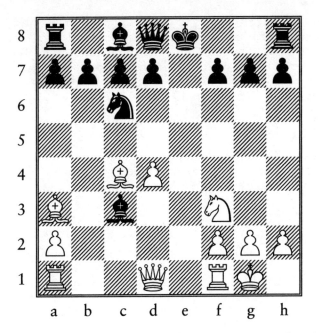

(c) Finally, **10 ... d6** is the line of longest resistance, but there is still plenty of attack left: *11* Rc1 Ba5 *12* Qa4! and there is no good defence to the threat of *13* d5 winning either the Knight or the Bishop.

Now let us return to the position at move eight: having convinced ourselves that *8 . . .* Nxc3 is too dangerous for Black, let us look at the alternative capture: *8 . . .* Bxc3 (see diagram overleaf).

At first sight, this might seem to solve all Black's problems. After *9* bxc3, he plays *9 . . .* d5! (not *9 . . .* Nxc3, which loses a piece to *10* Qe1+) and castles into safety next move, retaining an extra Pawn. But White has a beautiful way to interfere with this apparent logic.

9 d5!

White's Pawn occupies d5 before Black's can reach that square. Although Black has for the moment an extra piece, both Knight and Bishop are attacked by Pawns, and the Knight on e4 is also in some danger of being pinned along the e-file. Black must tread very warily if he is to avoid serious problems.

9 ... Bf6!

Some beautiful possibilities can result if Black unwisely tries to hang onto his ill-gotten gains with *9* ... Ne5 *10* bxc3 Nxc4. The key move here is *11* Qd4, attacking both Knights. There might follow *11* ... Ncd6 *12* Qxg7 Qf6 (*12* ... Rf8 *13* Bh6 is also bad for Black) *13* Qxf6 Nxf6 *14* Re1+ Kf8 *15* Bh6+ Kg8 *16* Re5! (threatening mate by Rg5) *16* ... Nde4 *17* Nd2! d6 (*17* ... Nxd2 *18* Rg5 mate) *18* Nxe4 dxe5 (or *18* ... Nxe4 *19* Re8 mate) *19* Nxf6 mate.

10 Re1!

The Knight on e4 is the more important for White to regain. Instead, *10* dxc6 bxc6 lets Black continue next move with *11* ... d5, supporting his Knight and attacking the Bishop.

10 ... Ne7
11 Rxe4 d6

This is a convenient place to terminate our analysis of the Giuoco Piano. Black will now quickly castle, retaining a single extra Pawn. White must think again about how to create some more attacking chances. Quite typically of many such violent attacking openings for White, Black's best strategy was to start by accepting everything thrown at him (the Pawn at e4, the Knight on c3) then, when the position began to become too uncomfortable for his King, to return the material, letting White take pieces back while Black was consolidating his defences. White's initial flurry of attack petered out, leaving Black safe with an extra Pawn, if still a little cramped.

We have dealt at some length with this analysis of the Giuoco Piano to give an idea of the depths to which one can pursue the investigation of a dynamic opening variation in which White tries to seize a strong initiative at the early stage. Despite spending several pages pursuing the possible variations, we have still only scratched the surface of the results of four centuries of analytical labour. In fact the whole idea of White's sacrificing two Pawns with 7 Nc3 and 8 0-0 was first investigated by the Italian master Greco in the sixteenth century. Yet there are still further discoveries to be made, and the volumes of chess literature devoted to opening theory should never deter anyone from pursuing his own researches and developing his own ideas.

Let us now move onto a brief survey of other open games related to the Giuoco Piano.

The Evans Gambit

After the characteristic Giuoco Piano *1* e4 e5   *2* Nf3 Nc6   *3* Bc4 Bc5, White has an extravagant possibility to give up a Pawn in order to gain time for quick development. Such a sacrifice in the opening is known as a **Gambit**, and the Gambit introduced by Captain W. D. Evans in 1826 is introduced by the move *4* b4 (see diagram overleaf).

White's idea is the same as in the Giuoco Piano: to play c3 and d4 to dominate the centre with Pawns. The point of *4* b4 is to lure the Black Bishop to b4, where it will be attacked by the Pawn when White plays c3. Sometimes, White will even be willing to invest more Pawns for the cause of quick development. For example: *4* . . . Bxb4   *5* c3 Ba5   *6* d4 exd4   *7* 0-0 dxc3   *8* Qb3 Qf6   *9* e5 and Black is very much on the defensive. More cautious players than Black will not grab the bait so eagerly, but will prefer to catch up with their own development by such moves as *7* . . . Nge7 instead of *7* . . . dxc3, or earlier to decline any material advantage by continuing *6* . . . d6   *7* Qb3 Qd7   *8* dxe5 Bb6 with a more solid game than in the Pawn-capturing lines.

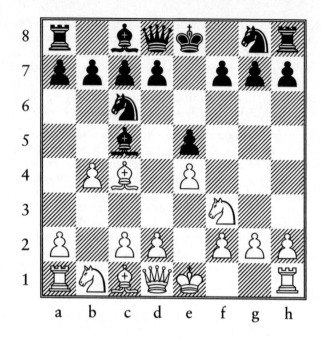

A beautiful White win from the Evans Gambit will be found in Anderssen–Dufresne among the illustrative games.

The Two Knights Defence

In both the Evans Gambit and the Giuoco Piano, part of White's play was motivated by the idea that the Black Bishop on c5 can be attacked by a Pawn coming to d4 or b4. But what if Black decides not to bring out that Bishop? Might it not be wiser, in fact, to develop the other Knight first? In that case, we arrive, after the moves *1 e4 e5 2 Nf3 Nc6 3 Bc4 Nf6*, at the Two Knights Defence.

The naming of chess openings is a colourful area. Some are named after their inventors or popularizers (Evans Gambit, Ruy Lopez, etc.), others after their countries or cities of origin (English Opening, Vienna Game, Dutch Defence, etc.), while some have purely descriptive appellations, such as the present Two Knights Defence. In general, the term 'Defence' is used to characterize a system introduced by Black's choice of move, while 'Opening' or 'Attack' is used for a White system.

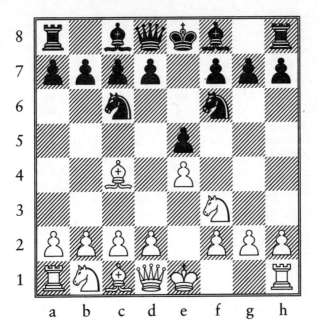

We have already met a game with the Two Knights Defence in Chapter 04, and it was not a happy experience for Black. The critical position arises after **4 Ng5** (taking advantage of Black's difficulties in defending f7) **4 . . . d5 5 exd5**. Now Black should not be in too great a haste to regain his Pawn. Having succeeded in closing the dangerous diagonal to f7, he should be wary about opening it again so soon. The most reliable move is **5 . . . Na5**, beginning the task of driving away the attacking pieces. Play might continue **6 Bb5+ c6 7 dxc6 bxc6 8 Be2 h6 9 Nf3 e4**, and Black continues to gain time and space by chasing the white pieces around. Alternatively, after **5 . . . Na5**, White could try **6 d3 h6 7 Nf3 e4** and Black again keeps the initiative since **8 dxe4** would lose the Bishop on c4. Note how in these lines it is Black who is playing a gambit, preferring to fight for the initiative rather than regaining his Pawn given up at the fourth move. If White does not like all this, he can, of course, play **4 d3** or **4 Nc3** instead of **4 Ng5**.

The Giuoco Piano, Evans Gambit and Two Knights Defence are the main openings that can be reached after the moves *1* e4 e5 *2* Nf3 Nc6 *3* Bc4, but they still do not exhaust the possibilities. Black can also play *3* . . . **Be7**, called the *Hungarian Defence*, which envisages a conservative but safe development plan with . . . Nf6, d6 and 0-0.

Finally, there is a jokey little move which, while not to be recommended, instigates a cunning trap: *1* e4 e5 *2* Nf3 Nc6 *3* Bc4 Nd4 *4* Nxe5 Qg5 *5* Nxf7 Qxg2 *6* Rf1 Qxe4+ *7* Be2 Nf3 mate! After Black's 4 . . . Qg5, White is already in great difficulties since *5* Bxf7+ Ke7 still leaves him with problems of how to defend his Knight without losing the Bishop. White's mistake here was to take the Pawn at move four. Instead of *4* Nxe5, either *4* Nxd4 exd4 *5* 0-0 or *4* c3 Nxf3+ *5* Qxf3 would leave White well-developed with the prospect of a good initiative before Black has brought his pieces into play. By playing 3 . . . Nd4, Black sets a trap, but if White sees through it then Black is committed to exchanging his Knight, which will have moved three times, for White's Knight which has only moved once. The resulting loss of time can prove a severe handicap in the race to prepare and launch an organized attack later in the game.

Now let us move on to some other openings after *1* e4 e5 *2* Nf3 Nc6. After the Two Knights Defence, we should mention the *Three Knights Game*, *3* Nc3, which turns into the *Four Knights Game* if Black maintains the symmetry with *3* . . . Nf6.

Most important, and most common of all open games in international chess, however, is the Ruy Lopez, named after a Spanish priest who published early analyses in 1561.

The Ruy Lopez   *1* e4 e5   *2* Nf3 Nc6   *3* Bb5

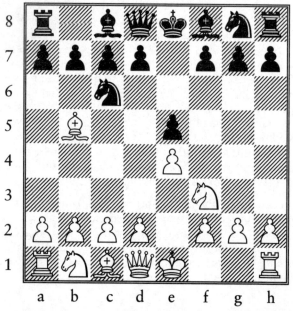

White adopts a more subtle approach than in the 3 Bc4 openings. The Bishop on b5 is placed where it can capture the Black Knight, or where it will pin the Knight in the event of Black's Pawn moving to d6 or d5. Since the Knight is defending the Pawn on e5, Black must think twice before allowing its exchange. In fact, the threat to the e-Pawn is, for the moment, illusory. After, for example, 3 . . . a6, if White plays 4 Bxc6 dxc6 5 Nxe5, Black cam immediately regain his Pawn with 5 . . . Qd4, attacking both Knight and Pawn on e4. In the resulting position, Black would have good scope for his Bishops. For that reason, White should not be too hasty in exchanging on c6. Let us continue the play:

    3 . . . a6
    4 Ba4 Nf6
    5 0-0

White hastens to bring his Rook into play. Now 5 . . . Nxe4 would carry some dangers for Black owing to the open e-file on which his King still stands. White could regain the Pawn at once with 6 Re1 (6 . . . f5 7 d3 or 6 . . . d5 7 Nxe5, exploiting the pin which has been latent since White's third move) or play even more aggressively with 6 d4!, hoping for more after 6 . . . exd4 7 Re1. So let us continue more cautiously for Black:

    5 . . . Be7

Black is now ready to castle and still has no need to worry about the loss of his e-Pawn: 6 Bxc6 dxc6 7 Nxe5 Nxe4 is quite comfortable for Black; the attack with 8 Qf3 Nf6 9 Re1 0-0 brings nothing.

    6 Re1

Now, at last, White threatens to win the Pawn. After the careless 6 . . . 0-0? 7 Bxc6 dxc6 8 Nxe5, Black remains a Pawn behind, since 8 . . . Qd4 9 Nf3 gives him no time to take on e4 with the Knight, while his Queen is attacked.

    6 . . . b5
    7 Bb3 0-0

With both sides safely castled, we can conclude our discussion of this opening. White's Bishop has ended up on this same diagonal as in the Giuoco Piano, but Black has been persuaded to adopt a more restrained posture than in that opening, with his own Bishop on e7. White appears to have lost some time, moving his Bishop three times to arrive at b3, but the real question is whether the moves a6 and b5 are advantageous additions to Black's position. They could easily give White something to attack by means of a4, and the further they advance unsupported, the more weak squares they are liable to leave behind them. If we continued our analysis, White's plan would be to increase his central presence with c3 and d4, then develop his Q-side pieces. Black finds it more difficult to play . . . d5, owing to the attack on his e-Pawn by the White Rook and Knight if White's own e-Pawn is exchanged. So Black will continue with . . . d6, then choose whether to develop his remaining Bishop on g4, e6 or b7 as he sees fit.

Before leaving the Open games, there is one more important possibility after *1 e4 e5 2 Nf3* which deserves a brief look. So far, we have only considered the reply *2 . . . Nc6* to defend the e-Pawn. Black can also, of course, defend with *2 . . . d6*, shortening the diagonal of one Bishop but opening the diagonal for the other. This is called *Philidor's Defence*. But there is another possibility which can lead to tricky play, with Black counter-attacking immediately against the white e-Pawn by bringing out his own Knight.

Petroff's Defence   *1* e4 e5   *2* Nf3 Nf6

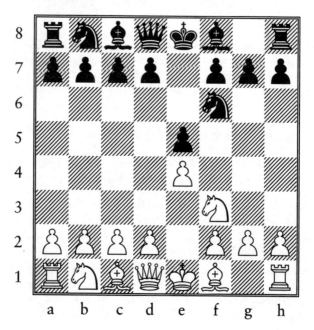

When something is attacked in a chess game, it is most usual to defend it or to move it away. Attacking something else in return is generally a dangerous recipe, and Petroff's Defence is no exception to this rule. After *3 Nxe5*, Black must be very cautious. The immediate *3 . . . Nxe4* would leave him in all sorts of trouble after *4 Qe2!*. As so often, the opening of the e-file with the Kings still in the centre acts to Black's disadvantage. Any retreat of the attacked Knight such as *4 . . . Nf6* or *4 . . . Nd6* would lose the Queen to a discovered check: *5 Nc6+!*. Even *4 . . . d5* would only postpone the decision about what to do with the Knight after *5 d3*. Actually, Black can cut his losses to a single Pawn by playing *4 . . . d5   5 d3 Qe7!   6 dxe4 Qxe5   7 exd5*, but that can hardly be counted a success.

In fact, the Petroff Defence is quite playable if Black is not in such a hurry to recapture his Pawn. After *3 Nxe5*, the right move is *3 . . . d6!* first chasing back the White Knight. Then after *4 Nf3 Nxe4   5 Qe2*, Black can defend and unpin the Knight with *5 . . . Qe7* when he stands in no immediate danger. But there can hardly be a more immediate demonstration of the potential problems of opening lines when the King is still in the centre of the board than that Queen-losing variation above. This Petroff trap must have claimed countless victims and will doubtless continue to snare unwary Queens for many years to come.

We have left unmentioned many more open games, but let that be enough for the time being. More comments on the openings with *1 e4 e5* will be found in the chapter of illustrative games at the end of this book. Let us move on to the semi-open games.

Semi-open games

After the move *1 e4* White will, if unimpeded, on the next move dominate the centre with *2 d4*. By controlling the squares c5, d5, e5 and f5, such a formation would make it hard for Black to find active squares for his pieces. The most common replies to *1 e4* are, therefore, those moves that inhibit White's d4 advance, or those which prepare to meet that move by establishing Black's own stake in the centre with *1 . . . d5*. Let us see how some of the popular defences conform to those ideas.

The Sicilian Defence 1 e4 c5

Apart from *1* . . . e5, the Sicilian Defence is the only reply to *1* e4 that prepares to exchange the White Pawn if it ventures to d4. Since *2* d4 cxd4 *3* Qxd4 only loses White time after *3* . . . Nc6, play often continues instead *2* Nf3 d6 *3* d4 cxd4 *4* Nxd4 Nf6 *5* Nc3 g6. Black prepares to complete the development of his K-side pieces with Bg7 and 0-0 (see diagram below). The black-squared Bishop then has a fine diagonal, and Black may also hope for activity for his Rooks along the half-open c-file. For the time being, however, the Pawn on e4 has a slightly cramping effect, restraining Black from occupying the d5 and f5 squares. In effect, White has four ranks for his men, while Black must be content with three. Besides *5* . . . g6, Black has another possibility of completing his development by playing *5* . . . e6 followed by Be7 and 0-0. The Pawns at e6 and d6 in such a position stand guard over the central squares c5, d5, e5, f5 and prevent White from increasing his command of space. The resilience of the Sicilian Defence and the proven opportunities for Black to counter-attack along the c-file in the middlegame have made the Sicilian one of the most popular of all defences to *1* e4.

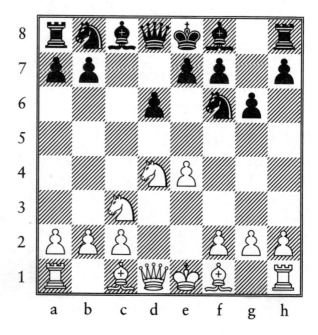

The next two defences we shall look at see Black allowing White's *2 d4*, but meeting it with *2 ... d5*. Since *1 e4 d5 2 exd5 Qxd5 3 Nc3* loses time for Black as his Queen is chased around, he needs to prepare d5 with a preliminary Pawn move. The two moves which fit the bill are *1 ... e6* and *1 ... c6*, and these are the next most popular replies to *1 e4* after *1 ... e5* and *1 ... c5*.

The French Defence   *1 e4 e6   2 d4 d5*

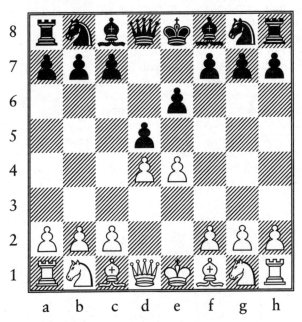

By playing *2 ... d5*, Black not only claims space in the centre, he also poses an immediate threat to the White e-Pawn. White must deal with this threat; he has three main options.

(*a*) Exchange Pawns with *3 exd5 exd5*. This relieves the central tension, but also solves Black's main development problem. His Bishop on c8, whose diagonal was blocked by the Pawn on e6, can now see daylight again.

(*b*) Pushing forward with *3 e5*. This blocks the central position and keeps Black's game cramped. Black's reaction should be to attack and try to exchange the central White Pawns with *3 ... c5*, followed perhaps by *... f6*, sniping at the cramping Pawns and forcing White to defend his extra space.

White controls more space but Black can take the initiative; a nicely balanced position.

(*c*) Defending the e-Pawn with 3 Nc3 (or 3 Nd2) and continuing to bring out pieces.

Finally it might be noted that 3 f3? is a mistake, though motivated by the sound idea of defending the e-Pawn. Unfortunately the weakening of the e1–h4 diagonal proves fatal: 3 ... dxe4 4 fxe4 Qh4+ and Black wins the Pawn on e4. After 5 g3 Qxe4+ he even wins the Rook on h1.

The Caro–Kann Defence *1* e4 c6 *2* d4 d5

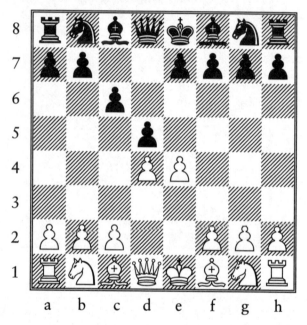

As in the French Defence, Black challenges the White e-Pawn. Again, White has three choices.

(*a*) 3 e5 does not have the same cramping effect as in the French position on the previous page, since the Bishop on c8 is free to move to f5, but the advanced Pawn still causes some congestion in the Black camp.

(*b*) Exchanging with 3 exd5 cxd5 again releases the central tension, but not with quite so symmetric a result as in the French.

(c) Defending the Pawn with *3 Nc3* maintains the tension and invites *3 . . . dxe4 4 Nxe4,* leaving White in control of a little more central space than Black.

In 1902, William Cook in his *Chessplayer's Compendium* described the Caro–Kann as 'A safe opening for a novice, but extremely dull'. Many modern players might agree with him, but chess is really too complex a game for any opening to be dull. If anyone wonders about the hyphenated name, incidentally, the opening was introduced by Herr Kann, of Pesth, and practised by Herr Caro, of Berlin.

That almost concludes our survey of the openings with *1* e4, but there are another two that ought to be mentioned as examples of the great variety of strategies that one can encounter even in the early stages of the game. We have so far considered only those openings in which Black immediately sets about challenging White's plans to dominate the centre with Pawns at e4 and d4. Until comparatively modern days it was almost unthinkable that any other approach was possible, but more recently systems have been developed which allow White to take hold of the centre, with Black relying on his ability to snipe at it later.

Two such defences are the Pirc Defence, *1* e4 d6, and Alekhine's Defence, *1* e4 Nf6. Let us see just one typical variation of each.

The Pirc Defence: *1* e4 d6 *2* d4 Nf6 *3* Nc3 g6 *4* f4 Bg7 *5* Nf3 0-0. Black has developed his K-side pieces satisfactorily and waits for a chance to hit back in the centre with . . . c5 or a well-prepared . . . e5.

Alekhine's Defence: *1* e4 Nf6 *2* e5 Nd5 *3* c4 Nb6 *4* d4 d6 *5* f4. Even more provocative, this defence invites the White Pawns forward in the hope that they will become objects of attack. After *5* . . . dxe5 *6* fxe5 Nc6, Black gains some initiative by putting pressure on the Pawns, but if White's centre does not collapse it may condemn Black to a terminally cramped game.

Strategies such as those of the Pirc and the Alekhine Defences demand great precision (and usually a great deal of theoretical knowledge also) and cannot be recommended to inexperienced players.

Closed games   1 d4 d5

Traditionally a more sedate way of opening the game, *1* d4 was largely ignored by both writers and players until early this century. Forthright attack was the only acceptable style of play and the slow manoeuvring games associated with *1* d4 were considered at the very least somewhat timid. As defensive play began to be better understood, however, and direct attacks brought less guarantee of success, slower methods of play became not only more acceptable, but a necessary adaptation to be made to every player's style. The emphasis shifted from all-out attacks against the opponent's King to an opening strategy designed mainly to control the centre and maintain active pieces.

The Queen's Gambit   1 d4 d5   2 c4

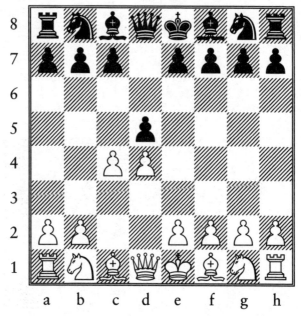

White tries in this opening to lure the Black Pawn away from d5, leaving White with a free hand in the centre. Experience shows that if Black takes the gambit Pawn, he cannot hang on to it. For example   *2 . . .* dxc4   *3* e3 b5   *4* a4 c6 (*4 . . .* bxa4   *5* Qxa4+ wins back the Pawn) *5* axb5 cxb5   *6* Qf3! is a drastic example of what happens if Black single-mindedly tries to defend his Pawn; the threat to his Rook costs him at least a Knight.

If Black does take the Pawn on c4, he is wise to let it be retaken shortly and just continue with his own development. A typical line of the *Queen's Gambit Accepted* might be **2 ... dxc4 3 Nf3 Nf6** (even here **3 ... b5** does not hold the Pawn: **4 e3 c6 5 a4 a6 6 axb5 cxb5 7 b3! cxb3 8 Bxb5+!** and the Bishop cannot be taken without Black losing his Rook) **4 e3 e6 5 Bxc4 c5**. Just as White has lured the Black Pawn away from d5, Black wants to exchange the central White Pawn. Both players will castle K-side and those decisive attacks are still a long way over the horizon.

Just as important as the Queen's Gambit Accepted are the variations where Black stoutly maintains his Pawn on d5, refusing to cede ground in the centre. After **1 d4 d5 2 c4 c6** we have what is known as the *Slav Defence*, while **1 d4 d5 2 c4 e6** is called simply the *Queen's Gambit Declined*. Note that **1 d4 d5 2 c4 Nf6** is a less logical method for Black to hold his central ground. After **3 cxd5 Qxd5**, he would lose time with the Queen when it is attacked by **4 Nc3**, while **3 cxd5 Nxd5** also loses Black time and space when the Knight on d5 is attacked by a Pawn moving to e4.

Let us examine one possible continuation of the Queen's Gambit Declined to see how play might develop:

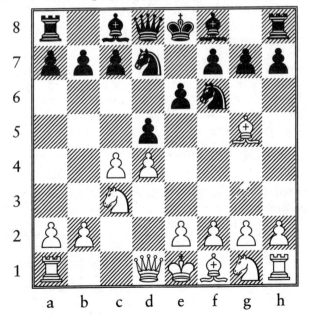

1 d4 d5
2 c4 e6
3 Nc3 Nf6
4 Bg5 Nbd7   (see diagram p. 147)

Black sets up a little trap. It seems that White can take advantage of the pinned Knight to win a Pawn by 5 cxd5 exd5 6 Nxd5, but Black has the surprising resource 6 . . . Nxd5! 7 Bxd8 Bb4+. White must give up his own Queen and remain a piece behind. Instead, play might continue 5 e3 Be7 6 Nf3 0-0 7 Rc1 c6 and Black firmly supports his centre Pawn. But he must still decide how he is going to bring out his undeveloped Bishop.

As we see, the early play is slower than in the 1 e4 e5 open games, with fewer direct threats and the hand-to-hand fighting postponed until a later stage of the game.

Semi-closed games

After 1 d4, Black may refrain from playing 1 . . . d5, but again his choices are mainly limited by the desire to prevent White from building his ideal centre with 2 e4. The only other Pawn move to prevent this advance is 1 . . . f5, the *Dutch Defence*, considered by many to be a little suspect because of the weakness it creates on the diagonal to Black's King. The principal Semi-closed games are the so-called **Indian Defences** beginning with the move 1 . . . Nf6. The usual reply for White is 2 c4, when the Pawns on c4 and d4 cover all the squares on the fifth rank from b5 to e5. White plans a massive take-over of space by his Pawns, with his pieces coming out behind them in support. Black must take care not to be deprived of all central space. The various Indian Defences each make their own claims to a central position for Black.

The Nimzo–Indian Defence: 1 d4 Nf6 2 c4 e6 3 Nc3 Bb4

Popularized by the great player Aron Nimzowitsch, after whom it was named, this opening restrains White in the centre while leaving Black's response flexible. The Bishop pins the White Knight making 4 e4 impossible (4 . . . Nxe4). Black can castle quickly, then decide what central Pawn formation he will adopt. He can still opt to advance his Pawn to d5 in Queen's Gambit

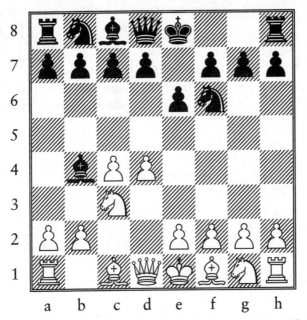

fashion, but another plan suggested by the move 3 . . . Bb4 is to exchange Bishop for Knight with Bxc3+, double White's Pawn on the c-file, then advance his own Pawns to d6 and e5. By exchanging his black-squared Bishop, Black gives himself the chance to coordinate his remaining forces with the Pawns on black squares to complement the remaining Bishop. Black would also hope to be able to attack the doubled Pawns later.

If White does not like the idea of his Knight being pinned in this Nimzo–Indian fashion, he can instead play 1 d4 Nf6 2 c4 e6 3 Nf3 when the move 3 . . . b6 gives us the **Queen's Indian Defence** (see diagram overleaf). The development of a Bishop on b7 or g7 was an idea which characterized the old Indian style of chess; openings involving this *fianchetto* development were therefore called 'Indian defences'.

White might answer with a similar Bishop development of his own, 4 g3 Bb7 5 Bg2 and play could continue 5 . . . Be7 6 0-0 0-0 7 Nc3. Note how the Black pieces control the centre from a distance, but Black stays prepared to advance with his Pawns to d5 or c5 when he is ready to challenge White's space-claiming Pawns on c4 and d4. Both armies are still keeping a respectful distance from one another and the real fight has yet to begin.

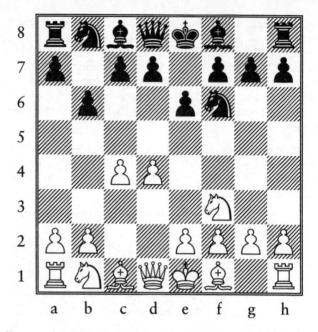

Finally, we should mention the **King's Indian Defence**, a more modern addition to Black's resources in which White is allowed full central occupation before Black stakes his own claim. The moves which characterize the King's Indian are Nf6 and g6 for Black with a later d6, aiming to put a Pawn on e5. Here is a characteristic King's Indian sequence: *1* d4 Nf6 *2* c4 g6 *3* Nc3 Bg7 *4* e4 d6 *5* f3 0-0 *6* Be3 e5 *7* d5. The armies are locked in conflict in the centre and both sides must make their plans for the middlegame. Black's most difficult problem is to find a role for his Bishops when the blocked Pawns have closed so many of the diagonals.

Flank openings

Last of all come the **Flank openings,** the slowest opening systems of all, in which White adopts a restrained development plan, often trying simply to control rather than occupy the centre, leaving the central Pawns at home, reserving them for later, much as Black does in many of the Indian Defences.

The most popular of the Flank openings is the **English Opening** *1* c4, which can easily lead into some of the Closed and Semi-closed openings which we have already discussed, if White later advances his d-Pawn alongside the c-Pawn. The English Opening received its name after the 1843 match in which the English Champion, Howard Staunton, defeated the strongest French player, Pierre Saint–Amant, in what was effectively a match for the world championship. Staunton's use of the then irregular opening move *1* c4 led to its being called the English Opening.

The most challenging reply is *1* . . . e5, taking hold of the centre squares which White has renounced. Play might continue *2* Nc3 Nc6 *3* g3 d6 *4* Bg2 Be6 *5* d3 g6 *6* e3 Bg7 *7* Nge2 Nge7 *8* 0-0 0-0.

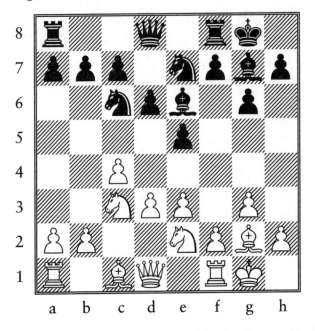

A typical English Opening position. White's Bishop on g2 has a beautiful view down the diagonal. White might consider continuing *9* Nd5 with a view to bringing the other Knight forward to c3, or he might prefer to prepare an advance of the b-Pawn with *9* Rb1 followed by b4 and b5. If the Knight can be dislodged from c6, the Bishop on g2 will be even more powerful.

So ends our very hurried trip through the major chess openings. There has only been time and space to give some of the characteristic moves of each and the principles behind those moves, but even this brief treatment may give some idea of the great variety of possible opening plans. Rather than trying to play all the different openings, it is generally a good policy to stick to a single White opening and Black defence in most of one's games, at least until one is ready to experiment further. Games which begin in the same way tend to continue in similar patterns. As one begins to recognize patterns repeating themselves, so one learns the strategic ideas behind the opening. In chess openings, familiarity breeds understanding.

08

illustrative games

In this chapter you will learn:
- how the ideas we have learnt have been put into practice in the games of the great masters of the past and present.

The origins of the game of chess are shrouded in some mystery, though north-west India has strong claims to be the scene of the birth of the game around the sixth century. Although the rules were somewhat different in those days, a game recognizable as chess was certainly played at that time, and is mentioned in two Sanskrit romances of the period. The game soon spread to Persia and Byzantium and by the time of the Middle Ages was beginning to be played in Europe.

In the early oriental forms of the game, the pieces had very limited powers compared with their modern moves. Knight and Rook retain their original moves, but Bishop and Queen were severely restricted. The Bishop was only allowed a two-square diagonal jump, while the Queen was permitted only a single diagonal move.

When the game reached Renaissance Italy, the rules were modified to make it more exciting. For nearly five hundred years, the rules have remained practically unchanged, but the game has developed from an idle pastime for the nobility into a highly researched science and international sport.

In this chapter, we shall follow the development of chess through the games of many of its greatest exponents. The games have been selected partly for their didactic value, but perhaps more for the beauty of their ideas and for sheer entertainment. In order to obtain the greatest value from playing through these games, a procedure that can be recommended is to recreate the moves of each game on a chessboard at least two times. The first time, a quick run through the moves and a cursory reading of the annotations should be enough to give a good feeling of what happened in the game. Then a more detailed and slower look at the moves will begin to give an idea of why it happened and particularly of how the early moves relate to what happened later in the game.

Game 1: Anderssen–Kieseritsky, 1851
King's Gambit

Until the second half of the nineteenth century, there was little organization of competitive chess. There had been many great players whose names have lived in history, such as the operatic composer and chess master Philidor (1726–95) whose feat of playing two or three games simultaneously, blindfolded, was hailed as 'a phenomenon in the history of man', but the games in those days were mostly offhand tests of ability, with perhaps some wagering on the side, but no formal prizes.

The first international tournament was organized in London in 1851, to coincide with the Great Exhibition of that year. Its instigator was Howard Staunton (1810–74), whose victory against Pierre Saint-Amant in 1843 had earned him the reputation of being the strongest player in the world. But the winner of the 1851 tournament was Adolf Anderssen (1818–78), the German champion whose dashing style produced many romantic and imaginative games. The present game was not played in the official tournament, but was an offhand encounter. Its dashing brilliance has earned it the title 'The Immortal Game'.

1 e4 e5   2 f4

This is the King's Gambit, most romantic of all chess openings. As in the Queen's Gambit, White tries to tempt the Black centre Pawn away to allow White to play d4. But the move 2 f4 also opens a line to the White King.

2 . . . exf4   3 Bc4 Qh4+   4 Kf1

White has allowed his King to be dislodged, but hopes to regain time by playing Nf3 attacking the Queen.

4 . . . b5

Characteristically for the chess of those days, Pawns are used as ballast, willingly thrown overboard in the fight for the initiative. Black distracts the Bishop from its attack on f7.

5 Bxb5 Nf6   6 Nf3 Qh6   7 d3 Nh5

Not only adding to the defence of the gambit Pawn on f4, but also carrying the threat to win Rook for Knight by playing Ng3+.

8 Nh4 Qg5   9 Nf5 c6   10 g4 Nf6

Black threatens both the Bishop on b5 and the Pawn on g4. Anderssen's reply is an imaginative idea to take advantage of the congestion of the black pieces on the K-side.

11 Rg1! cxb5   12 h4 Qg6   13 h5 Qg5   14 Qf3

White is a Bishop in arrears, but now threatens to trap the Black Queen by playing 15 Bxf4. Black's reply is designed to give the Queen a line of retreat.

14 ... Ng8   15 Bxf4 Qf6   16 Nc3 Bc5   17 Nd5! Qxb2
18 Bd6!!

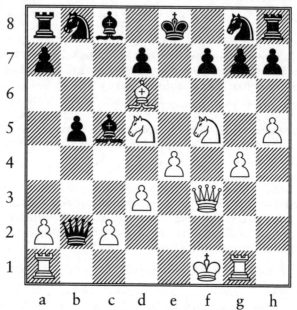

White ignores the attacks on both his Rooks. After 18 . . .
Qxa1+   19 Ke2 Qxg1 he would play   20 Nxg7+ Kd8   21
Bc7 mate.

18 . . . Bxg1   19 e5!

Cutting off the Queen's defence from g7 to renew the threat of
Nxg7+.

19 . . . Qxa1+   20 Ke2 Na6   21 Nxg7+ Kd8
22 Qf6+!! Nxf6   23 Be7 mate.

Anderssen's achievement in that game, sacrificing Queen and
both Rooks to force mate, is perhaps unparalleled in chess
literature, though a year later the same player came very close
to repeating the feat in another sacrificial orgy.

Game 2: Anderssen–Dufresne, 1852
Evans gambit

1 e4 e5   2 Nf3 Nc6   3 Bc4 Bc5   4 b4 Bxb4
5 c3 Ba5   6 d4 exd4   7 0-0 d3

Black's idea is to lessen the force of the attack by returning one Pawn. By refraining from the capture on c3, he also denies the use of that square to the White Knight.

8 Qb3 Qf6   9 e5! Qg6

Black cannot afford to capture on e5: 9 . . . Nxe5   10 Re1 d6 11 Nxe5 dxe5   12 Qa4+ costs him a Bishop.

10 Re1 Nge7   11 Ba3 b5

Both sides are fighting hard to gain the initiative. White has refused even to waste time by capturing on d3; Black now surrenders a Pawn in order to bring his Rook into the game along the open b-file, while also disrupting White's menacing formation of Queen and Bishop on the diagonal to f7.

12 Qxb5 Rb8   13 Qa4 Bb6   14 Nbd2 Bb7   15 Ne4 Qf5 16 Bxd3

White finally takes the Pawn. Now he has the threat of winning the Queen by a discovered attack: 17 Nd6+ or 17 Nf6+.

16 . . . Qh5   17 Nf6+

A move which completely changes many features of the position and suddenly exposes both Kings to great danger.

17 . . . gxf6   18 exf6

By comparison with the position just two moves previously, two files have suddenly become available for the Rooks to join the attack. The e-file is completely open, while the g-file is now available for a Black Rook. Notice too that with the disappearance of the Knight from e4, Black's Bishop on b7 has less in its way. Black's next move envisages a concerted attack against g2.

18 . . . Rg8

Played with considerable ingenuity. After 19 Bxe7 Qxf3 Black's attack could easily prove stronger than White's; any discovered check by the Bishop can be met simply with Kd8.

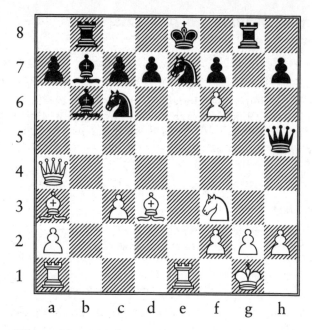

Many White players in this position would defend against the threatened capture on f3 by playing *19 Be4*, but Anderssen produced instead a combination of great beauty.

19 Rad1

This innocuous looking move conccals great venom. Black falls in with White's plans by taking the Knight.

19 . . . Qxf3   20 Rxe7+! Nxe7   21 Qxd7+!! Kxd7
22 Bf5++!

A double check, so Black has no time to capture the Rook or Bishop. He must move his King to escape both prongs of the attack. *22 . . . Kc6* is answered by immediate mate with *23 Bd7*, so there is only one move left.

22 . . . Ke8   23 Bd7+ Kf8   24 Bxe7 mate!

An amazing combination, particularly in view of the fact that White has for the last five moves been faced with the threat of mate himself. But let us return to the position of the diagram and look at just one more side variation. Suppose after *19 Rad1 Qxf3 20 Rxe7+* Black had simply moved his King away with *20 . . . Kd8*. Then there would have followed *21 Rxd7+! Kc8 (21*

... Kxd7 22 Be2+ wins the Black Queen) 22 Rd8+!!. Now Black can take the Rook in three ways, but they all lose either the Queen or the King: 22 ... Rxd8 23 gxf3; or 22 ... Kxd8 23 Be2+; or finally 22 ... Nxd8 23 Qd7+!! Kxd7 24 Bf5++ with mate by Bd7 next move whichever square the King runs to.

The most impressive move of this whole combination is Anderssen's 19 Rad1 which already envisages the final mating position. Note the role of this Rook in the play which follows and it becomes clear that Anderssen had based the move on a precise calculation of the mating positions.

After his victory in the London 1851 tournament, Adolf Anderssen had a strong claim to be regarded as the best player in the world. Soon, however, a player was to arise who would dominate the chess world to an unprecedented extent. That man was the brilliant American Paul Morphy (1837–84). Morphy's contribution to chess during his short career was enormous. He was the first to understand the importance of proper preparation before launching an attack. His contemporaries were mostly content to launch premature raids with whatever pieces were developed whenever the chance arose. Morphy saw that such attacks with inadequate force ought to be repelled. His own attacks were conducted only when he could call upon all his pieces to join the onslaught. Unlike most players of the time, he also knew how to win when a single Pawn ahead. He was even criticized in some circles for his willingness to exchange Queens and win the resulting endgames.

In 1858, Morphy crossed the Atlantic to do battle with the greatest European masters. He defeated all who would play him, including Anderssen, in set matches. But Morphy's most famous game was played not in an official match, but in the unusual setting of a box at the Paris Opera. To the accompaniment of Rossini's *Barber of Seville*, Morphy defeated two noblemen, consulting against him.

Game 3: Morphy–The Duke of Brunswick and Count Isouard, 1858
Philidor's Defence

1 e4 e5 2 Nf3 d6 3 d4 Bg4?

Already a mistake, for two reasons: firstly Black is compelled to exchange Bishop for Knight in an open position, and secondly the exchange loses time and brings the White Queen into the game.

4   dxe5 Bxf3

Black has no choice; *4 . . . dxe5* would have lost a Pawn after *5 Qxd8+* and *6 Nxe5*.

5 Qxf3 dxe5   6 Bc4 Nf6

Another error, defending against the threatened mate on f7, but allowing a double attack in reply. *6 . . . Qd7* would have been better.

7 Qb3!

Moving the Queen so much in the opening is rarely to be recommended, but here the double threat to f7 and b7 is full justification.

7 . . . Qe7

Having played the opening badly, the Duke and the Count now show resource in defence. After *8 Qxb7* they plan to bale out into an endgame with *8 . . . Qb4+*. Instead *7 . . . Qd7?* would have been far worse, since *8 Qxb7 Qc6* would save the Rook but lose the Queen to *9 Bb5*.

8 Nc3!

Morphy senses that he can try for a bigger advantage than a mere Pawn up in an endgame. White has already more pieces in play and Black must now spend another move defending his b-Pawn, while his Queen obstructs the development of the Bishop. While Black untangles, White can bring his remaining forces into play.

8 . . . c6   9 Bg5 b5

Motivated by a desire to drive back one of the attacking pieces, Black makes an error under pressure, but he was already hard pressed to find decent moves.

10 Nxb5! cxb5   11 Bxb5+ Nbd7   12 0-0-0

For the Knight he has sacrificed, White has turned the Black position into a pin cushion. Neither Knight can move and White threatens to win immediately with Bxd7+ or Bxf6 followed by a capture on d7. The Knight on d7 must be given another defender. Black would perhaps like to play *12 . . . 0-0-0* to escape from the pin, but that move would allow mate in two: *13 Ba6+ Kc7 14 Qb7* mate. There is only one alternative.

12 ... Rd8 (see diagram below)

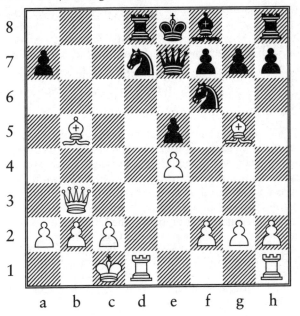

How is White now to increase his attack? Perhaps the natural plan might seem to be to play *13 Rd2*, followed by *14 Rhd1*, bringing the last Rook into play and bearing down with even more power on the pinned Knight on d7. Indeed, such a method of play ought to be enough to win, but Morphy, true to his style, forces the play to deny the opponent even a momentary respite.

13 Rxd7! Rxd7   14 Rd1

White's Rook joins the attack without delay. Nothing more can support the pinned Rook on d7.

14 ... Qe6

Now White can win easily with *15 Bxf6*, when *15 ... Qxb3* would allow mate by *16 Bxd7*, but perhaps Black might struggle on after losing his Queen with *15 ... gxf6   16 Bxd7+ Qxd7   17 Rxd7 Kxd7*. Instead, as before, Morphy finds the most elegant road to victory.

15 Bxd7+ Nxd7   16 Qb8+! Nxb8   17 Rd8 mate!

The economy of the final mating position is remarkable indeed.

The Morphy story had a sad ending. After defeating all in Europe on his grand tour of 1858–9, he returned to the United States and hardly ever played chess again. He may have been embittered at the refusal of Howard Staunton to agree to a match with him (by this time Staunton had effectively retired from serious play) but, whatever the reason, Morphy became less than positive in his feelings towards chess. He developed symptoms of paranoia and withdrawal, and died a solitary figure in his home town of New Orleans at the age of 47.

As players were learning to defend properly, and consequently also having to understand the importance of preparation in attack, strategy was becoming ever more important and the crucial decisions were delayed until later in the game. Everyone began to understand the value of patience and the art of winning long games. But in some far-flung outposts of the British Empire the spirit of the gambiteers lived on.

The last of our genuine antiques in this section of games is a particular favourite of the author. The winner, the Hon. R. Steel, was at the time a member of the executive council of the Viceroy of India. His opponent's name is not recorded. The game was played in 1886 in Calcutta.

Game 4: Steel–Amateur, 1886
Steinitz Gambit

   1 e4 e5   *2* Nc3 Nc6   *3* f4 exf4   *4* d4

More provocative even than the King's Gambit, this opening invites Black to harry the White King. In compensation, White has full control of the centre, but whether this is worth the indignity which the King has to suffer is difficult to justify.

   4 ... Qh4+   *5* Ke2

A modern player as Black here would be content now to play *5* ...d6   *6* Nf3 Bg4 with ... 0-0-0 and f5 to follow, disturbing the White centre and leaving the White King embarrassed in the middle of the board. The style of one hundred years ago, however, demanded more immediate measures.

   5 ...d5   *6* exd5 Bg4+   *7* Nf3 0-0-0

Black offers his Knight in the cause of rapid development and open lines.

   8 dxc6 Bc5   *9* cxb7+ Kb8

Rather than expose himself by taking the Pawn, the Black King shelters behind the White invader. Surprisingly, that White Pawn later plays a decisive role in the game.

10 Nb5 Nf6 *11* c3 Rhe8+ *12* Kd3

Black has mobilized all his forces, but has yet to break through to the White King. Now at last White is actually threatening to capture the Queen, since his last move unpinned the Knight.

12 ... Bf5+ *13* Kc4 Be6+ *14* Kxc5

White certainly seems to believe in leading with his chin. Objectively, *14* Kd3 would have been the only safe move, inviting a draw by *14* ... Bf5+. Now the White King hopes to reach safety via b4 and a3. White also still threatens the Black Queen, and he is now two pieces ahead. This remarkable position merits illustration.

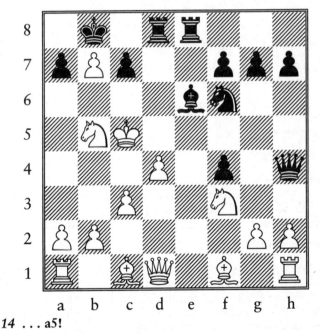

14 ... a5!

It is more important to deprive the White King of its flight square than to take time to worry about the threat to the Queen. Now *15* Nxh4 would leave White mated after *15* ... Ne4+ *16* Kc6 Bd5.

15 Nxc7! Qh5+ *16* Ne5 Nd7+

Black sees that *16 . . . Qxd1   17 Nc6+* would regain the Queen for White after *17 . . . Kxc7   18 Bxf4+* or *17 . . . Kxb7   18 Ba6+*. The Knight check played in the game intends to drive the White King to a less attractive square. Later it was discovered that *16 . . . Ne4+* might have been still more effective.

17 Kb5 Qxd1

Now *18 Nc6+ Kxb7* leaves White with no Bishop check on a6.

18 Bxf4 Qxa1   19 Ka6!

Suddenly the White King is transformed into a powerful attacking piece. The threat is *20 Nc6* mate, and *19 . . . Kxc7 20 Nxd7+ Kxd7   21 Bb5+* would also win for White.

19 . . . Nxe5   20 Nxe8

White threatens *21 Bxe5* mate. Black should now play *20 . . . Rd5*, but instead makes a plausible error.

20 . . . f6?   21 dxe5 f5   22 Be3!

When one diagonal is closed, the Bishop must find another. Now the mate threat is on a7.

22 . . . Rxe8   23 Bb5! Qxh1

Perhaps expecting White to take a draw with *24 Ba7+ Kc7   25 Bb6+ Kb8   26 Ba7+*, etc. But there is one final trick in the White armoury.

24 Ba7+ Kc7   25 Bc5

The threat is *26 Bd6+ Kd8   27 b8=Q+*.

25 . . . Rd8?

The correct move was *25 . . . Bc8!* when White has nothing better than a draw by checking endlessly on b6 and a7. Now Black has seen *26 Bd6+ Rxd6 27 exd6+ Kb8* or *26 Bb6+ Kb8   27 Bxd8 Qxg2* winning for him in both cases, but he has overlooked something more important.

26 Ka7! (see diagram) **Black resigned!**

A truly extraordinary final position. There is no satisfactory defence to the threat of Bb6 mate. Despite his extra Queen and Rook, Black is completely helpless. The White King, for so long an object of attack, finally has the last word.

With that remarkable game, we end our brief trip through the age of romantic chess. Our next game features the first official World Champion, a chessboard realist who dragged the game into the modern era. (Though as the inventor of the Steinitz Gambit, even he had a romantic side.)

Game 5: Steinitz–Tchigorin, Havana 1892
Ruy Lopez

After Morphy's withdrawal from active chess, Adolf Anderssen, winner of London 1851, resumed his reputation as the world's strongest practising player. In 1866 Anderssen lost a match to the Austrian champion, Wilhelm Steinitz (1836–1900), but the world still had to wait another twenty years for an official championship match. When Steinitz played Zukertort in 1886, the title of World Champion was at stake for the first time. Steinitz took the crown, which he wore with great glory for eight years. This game is from his last successful title defence.

1 e4 e5   2 Nf3 Nc6   3 Bb5 Nf6   4 d3

Whereas the earlier masters generally tried to open the position quickly as White, Steinitz was more often content to manoeuvre behind closed lines. Rather than rushing into action and relying on rapid development to secure an attack, the Steinitzian style was to prevent anything from happening until he was ready for it. His pieces would lie in ambush, waiting to counter-attack against an opponent who opened the position too early.

4 ... d6   5 c3 g6

A far-sighted move with three separate points: firstly, the Bishop is to be developed behind the Pawn, on g7 where it is out of the way of a later White central advance; secondly, the Pawn on g6 may support an advance of its neighbour to f5; thirdly, the square f5 is now unavailable for a White Knight. The relevance of this last comment will soon become apparent.

6 Nbd2 Bg7   7 Nf1 0-0   8 Ba4

White's moves create a curiously disjointed impression, yet they are part of a unified grand design. The Knight on f1 is heading for e3, eyeing the important d5 and f5 squares, while the Bishop prepares to retreat to c2, from where it will guard the e-Pawn after White advances d4. Note how the Bishop on b5 was pinning the Knight until the last move, effectively preventing Black's d-Pawn from advancing to d5 because of the reply Nxe5. Now that Black has castled, the Bishop returns to other duties.

8 ... Nd7   9 Ne3 Nc5   10 Bc2 Ne6

The Black Knights prevent White's expansion with d4, while Black himself hopes to advance his f-Pawn two squares to increase his control of the centre.

11 h4

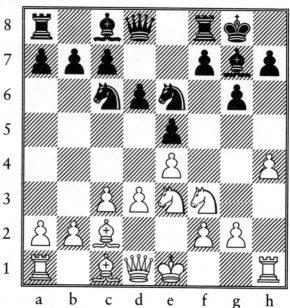

Steinitz's blueprint for attack at last reveals itself. Most players would have castled for White long before now, but Steinitz plans to use his Rook on h1 after opening a line by advancing the h-Pawn. His King will castle on the Q-side.

11 ... Ne7   12 h5 d5

In general, it is good policy to counter a wing attack by opening the centre. When the middle of the board is uncluttered, it is more difficult to concentrate one's attacking forces on the edge.

This recapture turns out to be a misjudgment. After *13 . . . hxg6*, Black would have had fewer problems on the diagonal a2–g8.

14 exd5 Nxd5   15 Nxd5 Qxd5   16 Bb3

The Bishop comes out of hiding onto a threatening diagonal.

16 . . . Qc6   17 Qe2 Bd7   18 Be3 Kh8   19 0-0-0 Rae8

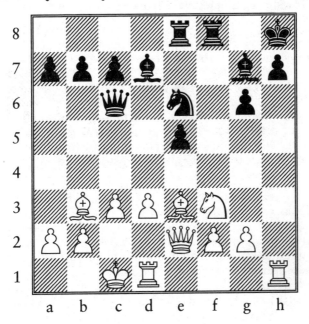

20 Qf1!

A move of great subtlety, the point of which only becomes clear after another four moves. Steinitz must already have envisaged the exchanges which follow, and the combination which wins the game for him.

20 . . . a5   21 d4!

At last this Pawn advances to its destined square, opening the game for White's attack.

21 . . . exd4   22 Nxd4 Bxd4   23 Rxd4! Nxd4

Black must have expected now 24 Bxd4+ Rf6, but a shock awaits him.

24 Rxh7+! Kxh7   25 Qh1+ Kg7   26 Bh6+ Kf6

If the King goes to h7 or h8 then 27 Bxf8+ is mate next move.

27 Qh4+ Ke5   28 Qxd4+   Black resigned.

It is mate next move: 28 ... Kf5   29 g4 mate. A game of great depth by Steinitz, with the Queen's entry into the attack via f1 and h1 only one of many pleasing features.

Wilhelm Steinitz had been the first man to attempt a proper scientific study of chess. Others before him had analysed the openings and endgames, but Steinitz subjected all phases of a game to the most minute analysis. Whereas previous commentators on games had generally been content to identify the fatal errors of the loser and praise the most imaginative moves of the winner, Steinitz's annotations sought to explain the game at a deeper level. His understanding of defensive technique and of the creation and exploitation of small positional advantages enabled him to claim to have established a 'general theory' of chess.

Steinitz remained champion of the world until his sixtieth year, finally losing to a man who had been brought up on his own writings. In fact, although Steinitz wrote about chess as an ordered logical system, his own play bordered on the eccentric. His faith in the defensibility of positions sometimes allowed him to adopt ridiculously cramped and under-developed situations, with deservedly bad results. But he was a stubborn man, who, in his later years, appeared to have faith in his abilities to defend the indefensible.

His successor as World Champion was Emanuel Lasker (1868–1941), one of the most rational players, both on and off the chessboard, that the world has ever seen. Lasker understood better than anyone, before or since, the stresses a player feels while participating in a serious game of chess. He was a versatile player who knew how to choose a type of position in which his opponent would feel uncomfortable. He understood the role of subjectivity in the choice of move. He would always play the man opposite as much as he was solving the problems posed by the board. The following game is an example of his subtlety of style.

Game 6: Lasker–Capablanca, St Petersburg 1914
Ruy Lopez

This game was played towards the end of a long tournament between the only two men who still had a chance of first prize. Capablanca was leading the event, so Lasker needed to win to overhaul him.

| 1 e4 e5 | 2 Nf3 Nc6 | 3 Bb5 a6 | 4 Bxc6 dxc6 |
| 5 d4 exd4 | 6 Qxd4 Qxd4 | 7 Nxd4 | |

Lasker's choice of opening variation is of great interest. Rather than choosing anything sharp and tactically complicated, he picks a system involving an immediate exchange of Queens. But the absence of Queens is by no means a guarantee of a draw.

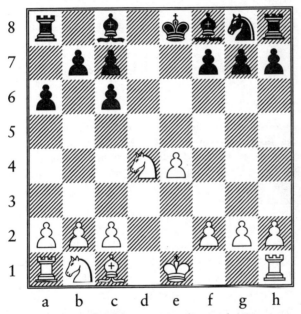

The key to understanding this position lies in the Pawn structure. White's majority of Pawns on the K-side can be advanced until a passed Pawn is created on the e-file. Black's majority on the opposing wing is crippled by the presence of doubled Pawns. This structural defect makes it impossible for him to force the creation of a passed Pawn. Indeed, if all the Knights, Bishops and Rooks were to vanish from the board, White would have every chance of winning the King- and Pawn-endgame.

In compensation for his crumpled Pawns, Black possesses the pair of Bishops which can be a powerful attacking combination if they can be made to work in unison. So Lasker's plan should be a gradual advance of the K-side Pawns, while Black might advance on the other wing to try to create space for his Bishops to work well.

7 ... Bd6   8 Nc3 Ne7   9 0-0 0-0   10 f4 Re8

The pin 10 ... Bc5 would have been met simply by 11 Be3. Now White must play with caution since 11 e5 Bc5 12 Be3 Nd5 favours Black, whose Pawns would be straightened out after 13 Nxd5 cxd5. White's next move avoids the awkward pin.

11 Nb3 f6

Played with a view to preventing White's e5 and hoping to fix the Pawn on e4 as an object of attack later in the game. Indeed, given a free hand, Black would continue with b6, c5 and Bb7, followed by Ng6 building up pressure against the Pawns on f4 and e4.

12 f5!

A move which totally alters the character of the position. White willingly leaves his Pawn on e4 backward in order to seize control of the e6 square. Forsaking the normal plan of creating a passed Pawn by playing e5, Lasker now relies on his Pawns to cramp the opponent and deprive his white-squared Bishop of much scope.

12 ... b6   13 Bf4 Bb7

An error of judgement, allowing a White Knight to become entrenched at e6. The correct plan was 13 ... Bxf4 14 Rxf4 Bd7 followed by Rad8 and Bc8.

**14 Bxd6 cxd6   15 Nd4 Rad8   16 Ne6 Rd7
17 Rad1 Nc8   18 Rf2 b5**

Black hopes to be able to bring his Knight to b6 and c4, but White's next move ties it to the defence of the d-Pawn.

19 Rfd2 Rde7   20 b4

A powerful move directed against the Black Bishop. Now 20 ... c5 would lose a Pawn for Black, so his Bishop must remain buried.

20 **... Kf7** *21* **a3 Ba8** *22* **Kf2 Ra7** *23* **g4**

White needs to open another front for his attack; the g-file must be made available for his Rooks.

23 **... h6** *24* **Rd3 a5** *25* **h4 axb4** *26* **axb4 Rae7**

The Rook can do nothing useful on the a-file, so returns to the centre. Now White sets about systematically preparing the further advance of his g-Pawn. If White's King stands on f4, and his Rooks on g3 and g1 when g5 is played, then the resulting opening of the g-file will leave White with a winning attack.

27 **Kf3 Rg8** *28* **Kf4 g6**

Black fights hard. Total passivity would be fatal against the plan of Rg1, Rdg3 and g5, opening the way for a mating attack with the two Rooks and Knight.

29 **Rg3 g5+** *30* **Kf3!**

An instructive moment. *30* hxg5 hxg5+ *31* Kf3 Rh8! would have left Black in charge of the open file. Now *30* . . . gxh4 *31* Rh3 wins back the Pawn, with the White Rooks ready to combine forces against the remaining Pawn on h6.

30 **... Nb6**

Still defending imaginatively. White must not be tempted by *31* Rxd6, which allows Black to get back into the game with *31* . . . Nc4 *32* Rd1 Ne5+ *33* Kf2 gxh4 and White's structure begins to collapse since his g-Pawn is under double attack.

31 **hxg5 hxg5** *32* **Rh3! Rd7**

After *32* . . . Nc4, White was ready with a neat trick: *33* Rh7+ Ke8 *34* Ra1! Rxh7 *35* Rxa8+ followed by *36* Ra7+ winning the Rook on h7.

33 **Kg3 Ke8** *34* **Rdh1 Bb7** (see diagram overleaf)

35 **e5!**

A neat sacrifice of a Pawn, clearing the e4 square for the Knight to enter the attack. Note how *33* Kg3 was played first to avoid the possibility of a discovered check with c5 in this position.

35 **... dxe5** *36* **Ne4 Nd5**

There is no other defence to the f-Pawn; *36* . . . Rf7 would allow a devastating check on d6.

37 N6c5

This move finally puts an end to the resistance. The attacked Rook cannot escape since, for example, *37 . . . Re7* *38 Nxb7 Rxb7* again allows *39 Nd6+.*

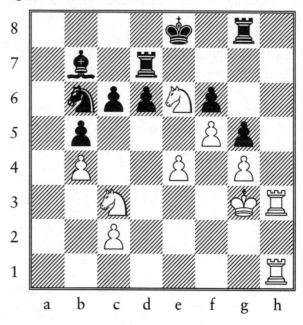

37 . . . Bc8 **38 Nxd7 Bxd7** **39 Rh7**

With Bishop and Pawn for a Rook, Black might normally be able to put up a fight, but the White Rooks retain all their attacking potential and the game is quickly concluded with a few more powerful blows.

39 . . . Rf8 **40 Ra1!**

The threat is mate in two, beginning with *41 Ra8+.*

40 . . . Kd8 **41 Ra8+ Bc8** **42 Nc5**

Now threatening any of Ne6+, Nb7+ or Rd7+, followed by Rxc8 mate. There is no longer any semblance of a defence.

Black resigned.

Although Lasker won that game and the St Petersburg tournament, he was to lose his title to Capablanca in 1921. José Raul Capablanca (1888–1942) acquired a reputation for invincibility at the chessboard. In the ten years following the St Petersburg tournament, he lost only one match or tournament game. His facility for avoiding complications by spotting danger well before it happened, combined with highly accurate endgame technique, enabled Capablanca to make chess seem too easy. Indeed, he even suggested that the game might be in need of more pieces and a larger board because it was becoming too dull. His fears have never been realized, needless to say, but in his best years, Capablanca did have the ability to play uncomplicated chess in a uniquely effective manner.

Game 7: Janowsky–Capablanca, New York 1916 Queen's Gambit Declined

1 d4 Nf6 *2* Nf3 d5 *3* c4 c6 *4* Nc3 Bf5 *5* Qb3 Qb6

Like Lasker before him, Capablanca was not averse to an early Queen exchange.

6 Qxb6 axb6 *7* cxd5 Nxd5 *8* Nxd5 cxd5
9 e3 Nc6 *10* Bd2   (see diagram overleaf)

Let us pause to look at the position for a moment. Black has allowed himself to be saddled with doubled, isolated Pawns. Are these not a weakness? They cannot defend themselves, it is true, but a Pawn is only weak if it can be attacked. White has little prospect of being able to do so: his Knight cannot manoeuvre to c4 or a4; the diagonal from g1–b6 is firmly blocked by Pawns; and it takes a long time before White can hope to play a Rook to c1, c3 and b3. In the meantime, Capablanca has already formulated a plan to utilize his doubled Pawns: the Knight is heading for c4, supported by a Pawn at b5.

10 . . . Bd7!

A marvellous move, paradoxically retreating the Bishop to a square where it will be locked in behind the Pawns. Black wants to play his Knight round to c4, supported by a b5-Pawn. For this to be carried out he wants the b5 square protected by the Bishop. Since he also wants to prevent White's opening the position with e4, Capablanca already envisages his f-Pawn coming to f5. Bearing all this in mind, d7 is the right square for the Bishop.

11 Be2 e6 *12* 0-0 Bd6 *13* Rfc1 Ke7!

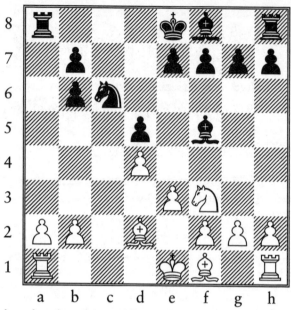

In such a closed position without Queens, the King is perfectly safe in the centre, so there is no need to tuck it away by castling. Indeed, had White thought about his moves instead of carrying out a routine development plan, he might have come to the same conclusion and posted his own King at e2.

14 Bc3 Rhc8   15 a3 Na5   16 Nd2 f5!

Alert to the possibility of e4, Black keeps the game blocked so that he can continue his Q-side manoeuvres in peace.

17 g3 b5   18 f3 Nc4!   19 Bxc4 bxc4   20 e4

Black has straightened his Pawns but now has to deal with the threat of e5, chasing his Bishop back. If White can secure the diagonal a3–f8 for his own Bishop, he would have an excellent position.

20 ... Kf7!   21 e5 Be7   22 f4 b5   23 Kf2 Ra4

Black has secured a bind on the position, but still needs something to attack. His first intention is to threaten b4.

24 Ke3 Rca8

Now the advance b4 is really threatened, since to capture the Pawn would lose White his Rook on a1.

25 Rab1 h6   26 Nf3 g5

Black has not lost interest in the Q-side, but having tied up White's Rooks on that wing proceeds to open another front on the K-side. He has plans to switch his Rooks over to the g-file.

27 Ne1 Rg8   28 Kf3 gxf4   29 gxf4

Of course 29 Kxf4 would have lost the Rook on c1 after Bg5+.

29 . . . Raa8

Black prepares to double Rooks on the g-file.

30 Ng2 Rg4   31 Rg1

31 Ne3 would have been of little use: 31 . . . Rh4   32 Rc2 Rg8 and the threat of 33 . . . Rh3+ is very awkward.

31 . . . Rag8   32 Be1 b4!

Just as White thinks that he has held the K-side attack at bay, and is even ready to drive back the invaders with h3, the Q-side storm breaks. Now the white-squared Bishop can join the game.

33 axb4

33 Bxb4 Bxb4   34 axb4 h5! leaves White helpless against the further advance of the h-Pawn. Holding it up with 35 h4 would then allow 35 . . . Rg3+   36 Ke2 Rb3 with great advantage.

33 . . . Ba4   34 Ra1

Instead 34 Rc1 (to keep the Bishop out of c2) could have been met by the surprising 34 . . . Rxf4+! 35 Kxf4 (or 35 Nxf4 Rxg1) Bg5+ winning back the Rook on c1.

34 . . . Bc2   35 Bg3 Be4+   36 Kf2 h5 (see diagram overleaf)

With the entry of this last Pawn into the attack, White can no longer hold his K-side together. The threat is simply h4, and White cannot untangle in time to deal with it. Even 37 Ne3 h4 38 Nxg4 hxg3+ 39 hxg3 fxg4 is hopeless for him. White's Rook is no match for the two Bishops, and Black quickly decides matters by invading with his own Rook via h8 and h2. Note how the Bishop on e4 prevents White from challenging the h-file.

37 Ra7 Bxg2   38 Rxg2 h4   39 Bxh4 Rxg2+   40 Kf3

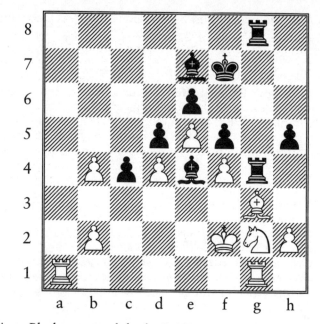

Since Black cannot defend e7 (40 . . . Re8 loses the other Rook), White has cut his losses to the exchange (losing Rook for Bishop or Knight is termed 'losing the exchange'), but the position is still hopeless in view of the strength of the Rooks and the prevailing weakness of the White King.

40 . . . Rxh2   41 Bxe7

41 Rxe7+ Kf8   42 Bf6 would have been met by 42 . . . Rgh8! when 43 Bxh8 Kxe7 is simple to win, while other moves allow R8h3 mate.

**41 . . . Rh3+   42 Kf2 Rb3   43 Bg5+ Kg6
44 Re7 Rxb2+   45 Kf3 Ra8**

Again threatening a two-Rook mate with Ra3.

46 Rxe6+ Kh7   White resigned.

47 Kg3 Ra3+   48 Kh4 Rh2 is mate.

While he was World Champion, Capablanca's effect on the development of chess was not wholly beneficial. His brilliance in exploiting small advantages seemed to have a deadening effect on the spirit of enterprise shown by his contemporaries. Would-be imitators of the great Cuban Grandmaster played with too great caution; at the highest levels, play was becoming too stereotyped and lacking adventure and risk. But two developments arose which were to bring back life to the game. Firstly, a group of young players grew up in central Europe who were to challenge many of the tenets of classical chess. These players, led by Richard Reti, Gyula Breyer and Aron Nimzowitsch, developed their own principles of centre control and Pawn-play which revolutionized opening theory and middlegame strategy. Their style became known as the 'Hypermodern' school, characterized by the development of Bishops in fianchetto on g2 or b2 (g7 or b7 as Black) and the delayed occupation of the centre by Pawns. The second development, which was to topple Capablanca, came in the shape of Alexander Alekhine.

Just as the hypermoderns resuscitated chess with the energy of their ideas, Alekhine (1892–1946) brought back to the game an energy of play characterized by a love of complications and an unparalleled will to win. His best games are enormous feats of control, with successions of combinations spanning the whole board. The following game is one of his most famous.

Game 8: Reti–Alekhine, Baden-Baden 1925
Irregular Opening

1 g3 e5   *2* Nf3

Reti always had a weakness for experimentation in the openings, particularly for the idea of playing Black defences with the white pieces, hoping to make something of the extra move. Here he tries an Alekhine's Defence with an extra g3, to enable quick development of the Bishop to g2.

2 ... e4   *3* Nd4 d5   *4* d3 exd3   *5* Qxd3 Nf6

6 Bg2 Bb4+

Black gives this check with his Bishop so that after 7 c3 Be7 White's Knight can no longer develop to its most aggressive square on c3. Reti refuses to cooperate with this plan, though his Knight still ends up on d2.

7 Bd2 Bxd2+   *8* Nxd2 0-0   *9* c4

With this move, White completes his opening strategy of eliminating the opponent's central Pawns. His Bishop on g2 finally has a free view along the long diagonal.

9 ... Na6 10 cxd5 Nb4 11 Qc4 Nbxd5 12 N2b3 c6
13 0-0 Re8 14 Rfd1 Bg4 15 Rd2 Qc8 (see diagram)

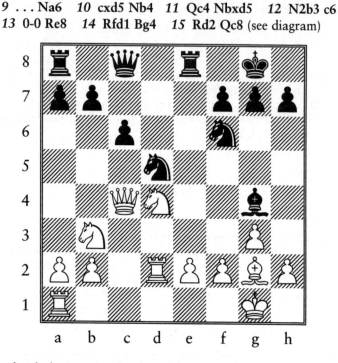

The battle begins to take shape: White is aiming for pressure against the Q-side Pawns with Nc5, while Black is trying to attack the enemy King with his pieces.

16 Nc5 Bh3!

Now after 17 Bxh3 Qxh3, the Black b-Pawn is undefended, but with the Black Queen so near his King, White cannot afford to take it: 18 Nxb7 Ng4 19 Nf3 (to defend h2) Nde3! 20 fxe3 Nxe3 and Black threatens both Qg2 mate and Nxc4. We can continue this variation with 21 Qxf7+! Kh8! (not 21 ... Kxf7 22 Ng5+ winning back the Queen) 22 Nh4 Rf8 and Black wins the Queen after all since any Queen move can be met by 23 ... Rf1+ forcing mate.

17 Bf3 Bg4 18 Bg2 Bh3 19 Bf3 Bg4

Black urgently wants to get rid of the excellent White Bishop, which White is just as keen to keep. Now 20 Bg2 would have enabled either player to claim a draw by threefold repetition of position, but Reti chose to keep the game going.

20 Bh1 h5

The fight is for the initiative. White has pressure on the Q-side which is hard to shake off. Any move of the Q-side Pawns by Black is liable to make matters worse, since advancing the b-Pawn leaves the c-Pawn hard to defend. The Pawns on c6 and b7 provide a useful buffer to the force of the distant White Bishop. Alekhine's plan is to create an attack on the other wing; his first priority is to weaken the position of the White King by advancing the h-Pawn and exchanging on g3.

21 b4 a6

A necessary defensive move. If White is allowed to play b5, too many lines of attack are opened on the Q-side.

22 Rc1 h4   23 a4

23 gxh4? would wreck the shelter around the White King and give Black a huge attack with 23 ... Bh3 followed by Qg4.

23 ... hxg3   24 hxg3 Qc7   25 b5

A perfectly natural continuation of White's plan, but as Alekhine brilliantly shows, it is too optimistic.

25 ... axb5   26 axb5 Re3!

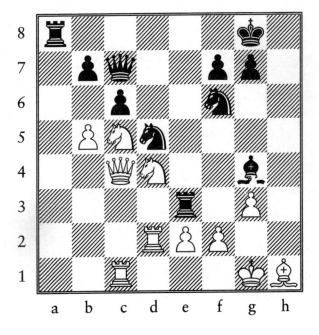

The culmination of the plan begun with *20 . . .* h5 and continued with *24 . . .* Qc7. The whole idea has been to weaken g3. Now it begins to show: *27* fxe3 Qxg3+ *28* Bg2 Nxe3 wins everything.

But this is only the beginning of the complications.

**27 Nf3 cxb5   28 Qxb5 Nc3   29 Qxb7 Qxb7
30 Nxb7**

Black had to calculate all this with great accuracy; his Rook on e3 is still attacked and its retreat would lose the Knight on c3.

30 . . . Nxe2+   31 Kh2

31 Kf1 would have been met by *31 . . .* Nxg3+ *32* fxg3 Bxf3. Now all the captures are satisfactory for White: *31 . . .* Nxc1 or *31 . . .* Bxf3 can be met by *32* fxe3, while *31 . . .* Rxf3 is answered by *32* Rxe2.

31 . . . Ne4!

Now almost every piece on the board is attacked. *32* fxe3 Nxd2 simply leaves too many white pieces hanging.

32 Rc4 Nxf2!

The only good move. Instead *32 . . .* Nxd2 *33* Nxd2! Rd3 *34* Nc5! would have left both Black Rooks and his Bishop attacked. Another wild possibility was *32 . . .* Bxf3 *33* Rxe4! Rxe4 *34* Bxf3, with advantage to White. Needless to say, it takes a very clear head to thread one's way through such a minefield of complications.

33 Bg2 Be6

Black has won a Pawn, but his attack rages on. The Bishop attacks a Rook while also vacating a square for the Knight.

34 R4c2 Ng4+   35 Kh3

The King must walk into a discovered check since *35* Kh1 Ra1+ would be fatal.

35 . . . Ne5+   36 Kh2 Rxf3!   37 Rxe2

37 Bxf3 Nxf3+ and *38 . . .* Nxd2 would have left White a clear Bishop behind.

**37 . . . Ng4+   38 Kh3 Ne3+   39 Kh2 Nxc2
40 Bxf3 Nd4**

Finally White's luck runs out. The Knight forks Rook and Bishop and after *41 Rf2 Nxf3+ 42 Rxf3 Bd5*, the Bishop forks Rook and Knight, winning at least a Knight.

White resigned.

Do not worry if the complications of this game seem beyond you on the first few times you play through it. Without doubt, the play from move 26 until the very end is one of the most remarkable, complex sequences of combinations ever recorded.

Alekhine defeated Capablanca for the world championship in 1927 and, apart from a brief spell between 1935 and 1937, held the title until his death in 1946. From Steinitz until Alekhine, there had been no systematic design of competition for the world championship. Matches were sporadic, occurring only when public pressure and financial considerations forced the champion to defend his title against an aspiring challenger. Some of the greatest players of the era never had a chance to play for the world championship, simply because they could not raise the finances necessary to tempt the champion into risking his crown. Indeed, Alekhine himself was accused of avoiding his most dangerous rivals; his refusal to grant Capablanca a return match aroused particular criticism.

With the death of Alekhine, however, the opportunity was taken to introduce some order into the system. The International Chess Federation had already been in existence for some years, but only now managed to take control of the international game. In 1948 a tournament was arranged to decide who would take the place left vacant by Alekhine. The eventual winner was Mikhail Botvinnik (1911–95), who became the first of a long line of world champions from the Soviet Union.

Game 9: Botvinnik–Capablanca, AVRO 1938
Nimzo–Indian Defence

The AVRO tournament, held in Holland in 1938 under the sponsorship of the Dutch wireless company Algemene Verenigde Radio Omrep, gathered together the eight greatest players in the world in an attempt to produce a winner to challenge Alekhine. Three players of the younger generation in fact finished ahead of the World Champion. Keres (Estonia) and Fine (USA) shared first place, with Botvinnik (USSR) third. Capablanca could manage only seventh place. The outbreak of war prevented any title match, and by the time the world was at peace again, Botvinnik had outdistanced all rivals with games of huge strategic power such as this one.

1 d4 Nf6   2 c4 e6   3 Nc3 Bb4   4 e3

It looks a little odd for White to shut in his Q-Bishop in this manner, but there are two good reasons to do so: first, with the pin on the Knight, White does not want his Bishop to stray too far from defence of the a5–e1 diagonal; second, and more deeply, White has visions of preparing a later e4, re-opening the diagonal. We shall see how far-sighted this idea really is as the game progresses.

4 ... d5   5 a3 Bxc3+   6 bxc3

After Black has played d5, White is happier allowing the doubling of his Pawns, since he knows that he can always exchange the front c-Pawn.

6 ... c5

With White still undeveloped, Black is happy to open the game with Pawn exchanges. He need not fear 7 dxc5, since White can hardly hope to maintain his extra Pawn. After 7 ... Qa5, for example, Black attacks two of the c-Pawns and 8 Qd4 Nc6 would not long delay the recapture of the Pawn.

7 cxd5 exd5   8 Bd3 0-0   9 Ne2

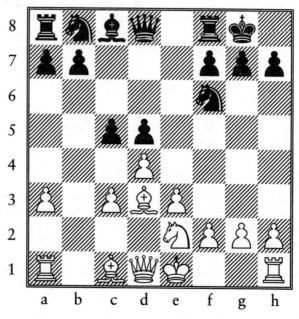

The Knight develops behind the Pawns in order not to impede their later advance. White's Bishop on c1 still yearns for an open diagonal, so the plan is to advance f3 and e4. If Black guards the e4 square to prevent that advance, then the Knight can move from e2 to g3 to add its support. These considerations make the move 9 Ne2 far more attractive than the superficially more aggressive Nf3.

> **9 ... b6   10 0-0 Ba6**

Black plays to exchange the more active of the two White Bishops. After the exchange, if White's Pawns remain fixed on black squares, the Black Knight will prove superior to the White Bishop.

> **11 Bxa6 Nxa6   12 Bb2**

The Bishop gets out of the way in order to allow the Rook to develop from a1.

> **12 ... Qd7   13 a4**

White must take care if he is not to have his white squares invaded. The careless 13 Qd3 Qa4 would have paralysed White on the Q-side.

> **13 ... Rfe8   14 Qd3 c4**

A highly committal decision by Black which changes the nature of the position by blocking the Pawns. His plan is to bring the Knight round to b3 in order eventually to win the Pawn on a4. Meanwhile, however, the relaxation of the tension gives White a freer hand in the centre.

> **15 Qc2 Nb8   16 Rae1 Nc6   17 Ng3 Na5   18 f3 Nb3**
> **19 e4 Qxa4**

White has achieved his planned central advance, Black has won his Pawn. Now White must push forward on the K-side before Black's Q-side Pawns rush onwards.

> **20 e5 Nd7   21 Qf2 g6   22 f4 f5**

This advance, prepared by his previous move, prevents White's automatic space-gaining plan with f5, followed by further Pawn pushes to open lines to the Black King.

> **23 exf6 e.p. Nxf6   24 f5 Rxe1   25 Rxe1 Re8**

Black plays to exchange all the Rooks, lessening White's potential power on the open lines on the K-side.

26 Re6! Rxe6   27 fxe6 Kg7   28 Qf4

White's 26th move has given him a passed Pawn which also helps the attack against the King. Now besides having to worry about Qc7+, Black is faced with such attacking possibilities as 29 Nf5+ gxf5 30 Qg5+ followed by Qxf6+ wherever the King moves. It is time for Black's Queen to return to the defence.

28 . . . Qe8   29 Qe5 Qe7

Black seems to have held his game together; the passed e-Pawn is blockaded and the Knight on f6 securely protected. The Knight on b3 performs the important duty of preventing the Bishop from reclaiming its rightful diagonal on c1. White must find a way to add fuel to his attack.

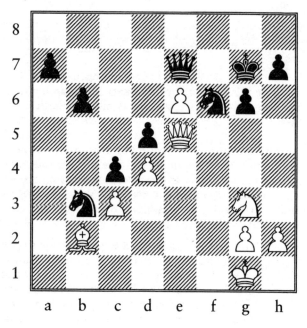

30 Ba3!

The Black Queen is lured away in order to deprive the King of a necessary defender. The Bishop sacrifice is just a prelude to another offer.

30 . . . Qxa3   31 Nh5+ gxh5

The pinned Knight, of course, cannot capture.

32 Qg5+ Kf8   33 Qxf6+ Kg8   34 e7

White has carefully calculated that the following Black checks lead to nothing. Instead, he might also have played *34 Qf7+ Kh8   35 h3!*, giving the King a safe place to hide on h2 and leaving Black defenceless against the further advance of the Pawn to e7 and e8.

**34 ... Qc1+   35 Kf2 Qc2+   36 Kg3 Qd3+
37 Kh4 Qe4+   38 Kxh5**

Black's problem is that when the checks run out he cannot defend against both Qf8 mate and e8=Q.

38 ... Qe2+   39 Kh4 Qe4+   40 g4 Qe1+   41 Kh5 resigns.

A very pleasingly logical game, with White's long-planned advance in the centre paving the way for the decisive attack against the King.

When Botvinnik took the world championship title to the USSR, it was a long time before any other nation had even a glimpse of it. Until the Soviet Revolution, chess had just been a harmless pursuit of the thinking classes. Lenin's advocacy of the game turned it into a means of mass culture and education, a propaganda weapon and, above all, an organized sport on a massive scale. With millions of chessplayers competing in tournaments in the USSR, the level of play rose enormously, and at the top levels the game was being studied as never before. The generation of Soviet players which arose during the war years was to dominate the world game for a quarter of a century.

Botvinnik himself never established a proper superiority over the other leading players in tournament play, but in matches for his title he proved to be a stubborn and very dangerous opponent. The new rules for the world championship specified a title match every three years, the champion having to defend against the winner of a long series of eliminating contests. If he lost his title, the ex-champion had the right to a return match the following year. Botvinnik often seemed to use the first match to size up his opponent. If he lost, it was all valuable material for his astute preparation for the return match. In this manner, Botvinnik twice lost then regained his title, against Smyslov in 1957–8 and against Tal in 1960–1. In other defences of his title, in 1951 and 1954, Botvinnik kept his crown by drawing matches with Bronstein and Smyslov. As World Champion, he never actually won a match for the championship, but as ex-champion he was highly successful in the task of regaining it.

Of all his opponents in this period, Vasily Smyslov (b. 1921) was the most consistently dangerous to Botvinnik. At his best, Smyslov's play has a subtlety which few have been able to match. Here is just one example of his skill in exploiting small advantages.

Game 10: Smyslov–Benko, Monaco 1969
English Opening

1 c4 c5   2 Nf3 Nf6   3 g3 g6   4 b3

White employs a thoroughly hypermodern opening, leaving the advance of his centre Pawns until later.

4 ... Bg7   5 Bb2 b6   6 Bg2 Bb7   7 0-0 0-0   8 Nc3

White's unpretentious set-up poses Black no direct problems, except for a nagging awareness that he will always be one move behind as long as play continues symmetrically. Black's response is to initiate a series of exchanges which at first glance lead to total sterility, but on closer inspection actually leave White with some advantage.

8 ... d5   9 Nxd5 Nxd5   10 Bxg7 Kxg7
11 cxd5 Qxd5   12 d4 cxd4   13 Qxd4+ Qxd4
14 Nxd4 Bxg2   15 Kxg2

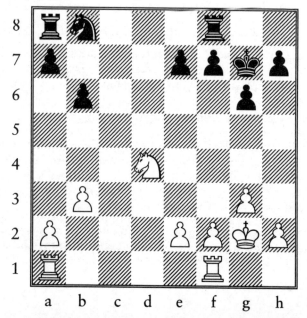

A player of an earlier generation would have been horrified to see the way White has handled the opening: no attempt to attack, just encouraging exchange after exchange. Yet this endgame is precisely what Smyslov had in mind when planning his opening strategy. The Knight on d4 is well-placed to attack the Q-side Pawns from b5 or c6, and White's Rooks are ready to occupy the open files and infiltrate into Black's position.

15 ... Rc8   16 Rac1 Nd7   17 Rfd1 Nc5   18 b4 Na4 19 Nb5

Black is already in difficulties. The threat is *20 Rxc8 Rxc8 21 Nxa7*, winning a Pawn. *19 ... a6* does not help, because after *20 Nc7* White wins material anyway: *20 ... Rb8   21 Nxa6* or *20 ... Ra7   21 Ne6+!*

19 ... Rxc1   20 Rxc1 a5   21 a3 Rd8   22 Rc7 Rd5 23 Na7 axb4   24 axb4 e6   25 Nc6

Black has managed to safeguard his Q-side Pawns, but now the other wing comes under fire. White threatens *26 e4*, expelling the Rook from d5 in order to be able to play either Nd8 or Ne5, with a further attack on the f-Pawn. Both White's Rook and Knight are more active than their Black counterparts, and if the Black Knight moves from a4, White can return his attention to attacking the b-Pawn with Rb7.

25 ... Rd2

Black puts his faith in counter-attack.

26 Ne5 Rxe2   27 Nxf7 h5   28 Ng5+ Kf6   29 Kf1!

A neat way to put a finishing touch to the game. After *29 ... Rb2   30 f4!* Black cannot avoid mate. The threat is *31 Rf7* mate, and *30 ... Kf5   31 h3* completes the net around the Black King.

29 ... Rxf2+   30 Kxf2 Kxg5   31 Ke3

White can use his King and Rook to attack Pawns which the cumbersome Black Knight cannot effectively defend. The win is no longer difficult.

31 ... Kg4   32 b5 Kh3   33 Rc4 Nb2   34 Rc2   Black resigns.

After *34 ... Na4   35 Kf4 Nc5* White wins most simply with *36 Rxc5 bxc5   37 b6*: White obtains a new Queen long before any Black Pawn becomes dangerous. Equally, after

34 ... Nd1+, White has the choice between winning the Knight with *35* Ke2 or ignoring it with *35* Kf3 and continuing with Rc6 and Rxb6, when the b-Pawn again wins easily.

The remarkable feature of that game was not so much the polished technique in winning the endgame with a small advantage, but the very conception at the outset that such an advantage could even exist after the many piece exchanges. Such powerful insights into a position are what has throughout the development of chess marked the games of the greatest masters. Of course, once Smyslov had shown the way with a victory such as this, many lesser mortals were able to learn the strategy and win their own subtle endgames with pale carbon copies of the same procedure. In such a manner the general level of chess technique is always rising, with the great players producing new ideas and new strategies, and the lesser masters learning all the time from their betters.

Returning to our procession of Soviet world champions, Botvinnik was finally persuaded to relinquish the title for good in 1963, when he was defeated by Tigran Petrosian (1929–84). The clause in the regulations which had previously allowed the defeated champion a return match had by now been abolished, so Botvinnik was permanently relegated to the sidelines. Petrosian held the title for six years, finally losing to Boris Spassky (b. 1937) in 1969. Whereas Petrosian had been famed for his ability to manoeuvre in closed positions, Spassky brought back the flavour of classical attacking play in open positions.

Game 11: Larsen–Spassky, Belgrade 1970 Larsen's Opening

Belgrade 1970 was the scene for one of the greatest chess spectaculars in history. A team from the USSR, which included five past or present world champions, met a team from the Rest of the World. The match was a win by the narrowest of margins to the USSR. On second board, Petrosian was defeated 3–1 by Bobby Fischer; while on first board, Boris Spassky met the Danish Grandmaster Bent Larsen, who had been the winner of a string of recent international tournaments. Honours ended even between these two great players, but Larsen's defeat in the present game was a beautiful miniature.

1 **b3**

A relatively unexplored opening move which gives Black a totally free choice in formation to adopt.

1 . . . e5   2 Bb2 Nc6   3 c4 Nf6   4 Nf3

White provocatively allows his Knight to be attacked by the Black Pawn. His idea is that the advance of that Pawn will open the diagonal again for the Bishop on b2. Spassky accepts the challenge.

4 . . . e4   5 Nd4 Bc5   6 Nxc6 dxc6   7 e3 Bf5
8 Qc2 Qe7   9 Be2 0-0-0   10 f4

Black has developed all his men energetically and must now decide upon a plan of attack. His grip on the d3 square makes it impossible for White to advance his d-Pawn (it would be taken en passant if it advanced to d4), so the Pawn on e4 virtually cuts the board in half. This should give Black the idea of launching a concerted attack on the White King, since White's forces will find it difficult to come to the defence from the Q-side of the board.

10 . . . Ng4!

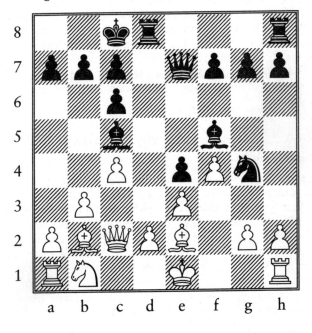

Now after *11* Bxg4 Bxg4, White totally loses control of d3. Black could even make life worse by playing *11* . . . Qh4+! *12* g3 Qxg4, leaving the K-side a mass of white-squared weaknesses. But the move *10* . . . Ng4 is based upon a far deeper and more imaginative analysis of the combinative possibilities. One variation which must have passed through Spassky's mind here is the following: *11* Nc3 Rxd2! *12* Qxd2 (or *12* Kxd2 Bxe3+ *13* Kd1 Rd8+ *14* Ke1 Bf2+ with a similar outcome) *12* . . . Bxe3 *13* Qc2 (or *13* Qd1) *13* . . . Bf2+ with Ne3+ to follow, winning the Queen. The ease with which Black blasts his way through the apparently solid White formation in this line is quite remarkable.

11 g3 h5!

The Rook on h8 wants to join the attack as soon as possible.

12 h3 h4!

Black's attack works in this game simply because more pieces can rush to aid the onslaught than are able to help the defence. He is therefore justified in sacrificing material to open lines. Of course, this is easy to write after the game, but at the time such intuition, however logical, needs supporting by hard analysis of precise possibilities.

13 hxg4

13 Bxg4 Bxg4 *14* hxg4 hxg3 leads to a very similar finish to that of the game.

13 . . . hxg3 *14* Rg1

Hoping to keep out the Black Rook from h1. Instead *14* Rxh8 Rxh8 leaves White immediately defenceless to the K-side threats; *15* gxf5 Rh1+ *16* Bf1 g2 and all is over.

14 . . . Rh1!!

A beautiful culmination of the attack. The Rook is given up to gain time for the Pawn to advance.

15 Rxh1

15 Kf1 Rxg1+ *16* Kxg1 Qh4 is just as final; there is no defence to the threat of *17* . . . Qh2+ *18* Kf1 Qf2 mate.

15 . . . g2 *16* Rf1

After *16* Rg1, Spassky had planned *16* . . . Qh4+ *17* Kd1 Qh1! and the g-Pawn again triumphs.

16 ... Qh4+   *17* Kd1 gxf1=Q+

Forcing mate in at most three moves: *18* Bxf1 Bxg4+   *19* Be2 Qh1 mate or *19* Kc1 Qe1+   *20* Qd1 Qxd1 mate.

White resigned.

Such brevity is a great rarity in modern chess, but the precision of the attack is admirable. Note how White was just one move away from being able to castle Q-side out of danger; he just never had the chance to move the Q-Knight.

Despite his brilliant career both before and after winning the world championship, Boris Spassky seems destined to be remembered most for having been the man who lost to Bobby Fischer. The most famous and chaotic world championship match was held in Reykjavik in 1972, when the extraordinary American Grandmaster Bobby Fischer came to wrest the crown from the Russians. Fischer's behaviour before the match had been an almost endless series of disputes with the organizers concerning the conditions of play, finances, regulations for filming the games, even the colours of squares on the chessboard. Many times the negotiations were on the point of total breakdown. Ultimata were delivered and ignored. The match was postponed, but finally Fischer and Spassky met across the board. Amid unparalleled press and television coverage and extraordinary tension, Spassky won the first game. Then Fischer failed to turn up for the second and lost by default. To everyone's surprise, the American returned for game three and won a brilliant victory. After that nothing could stop him. For the first time since the war, a non-Russian was the World Chess Champion. Here is the sixth game of their match, the game in which Fischer took the lead, which he was never to relinquish.

Game 12: Spassky–Fischer, Reykjavik 1972
Queen's Gambit Declined

1 c4 e6   *2* Nf3 d5   *3* d4

Although the game started as an English Opening, *1* c4, we are now in a position which would have been expected after the moves *1* d4 d5   *2* c4 e6   *3* Nf3. Thus the opening is termed a Queen's Gambit since the position reached is characteristic of that variation.

3 ... Nf6   *4* Nc3 Be7

After *4* . . . dxc4, White could regain the Pawn either by *5* Qa4+ or *5* e3. Spassky prefers to keep his Pawn in the centre of the board.

5 Bg5 0-0   6 e3 h6   7 Bh4 b6

With the Pawn on e6 blocking the Bishop, this Pawn move opens the possibility of developing it actively on b7.

8 cxd5 Nxd5   9 Bxe7 Qxe7   10 Nxd5 exd5   11 Rc1

White's exchanges have left the Pawn firmly blocked on d5, so there is less future now for the Bishop on the b7 diagonal. Meanwhile, the c8–h3 diagonal has become unblocked so, with his next move, Black changes course again. Note that White does not fear *11* . . . Qb4+ since *12* Qd2 Qxd2+ *13* Kxd2 would leave the Rook on c1 bearing down uncomfortably on the Pawn on c7 – a backward Pawn on a half-open file.

11 . . . Be6   12 Qa4 c5

Now we can see the other role of the move 7 . . . b6; the Pawn on that square supports the advance of its neighbour to c5.

13 Qa3 Rc8

Let us pause to look at the characteristics of the position after the opening has been completed. The main focus of attention is the Black Pawn on c5, attacked and defended three times, and pinned along the diagonal from a3 to e7. If Black can succeed in unpinning his Pawn, then he might hope to advance it to c4, then advance also the b-Pawn and a-Pawn to create a mobile mass of Pawns on the Q-side. Indeed Black's majority of Pawns on that wing could become a strong force. White, of course, does not have to allow this. He is happy to maintain the pin, as long as it ties Black down, but he can always take the force out of the Pawns by exchanging on c5 with dxc5. The question is whether Black will be able to make any advantage out of the open b-file which would result from his recapturing with the b-Pawn.

14 Bb5 a6   15 dxc5 bxc5   16 0-0 Ra7

At last Black threatens to capture the Bishop on b5, since his Rook is now defended by the Queen.

17 Be2 Nd7   18 Nd4

White takes full advantage of the possibilities of the pin in this game. Now Black cannot take the Knight without losing his Queen.

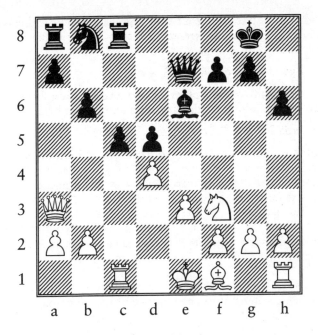

18 ... Qf8 *19* Nxe6 fxe6 *20* e4!

White is playing to open lines for his Bishop, to prove that it is superior to the Black Knight. Black is unwilling to play *20* ... dxe4, since that would leave him with four isolated Pawns (a6, c5, e4 and e6) all vulnerable to attack. White could continue *21* Rc4 Qf5 *22* Ra4 Rca8 *23* Qe3 Nf6 *24* Rc1 and one of the Pawns must finally fall, leaving three weak and still in need of constant attention. Note how White attacks the a-Pawn in this line, and the exploitation of its vulnerability on a6. With such ideas in mind Fischer played the Bishop to b5 on move 14, sensing that the Pawn would be more easily attacked if it could be induced to advance one square.

20 ... d4

Black gives himself a passed Pawn, but one which has little hope of advancing any further since d3 is firmly under the control of the White Bishop. Now that Bishop has a beautiful square on c4, but first the weakness on e6 must be fixed.

21 f4 Qe7 *22* e5 Rb8 *23* Bc4 Kh8 *24* Qh3

The attack on e6 begins to force Black into total passivity. Black can hardly consider *24* ... Rxb2 *25* Bxe6, after which he would be subjected to a ferocious attack by Rce1 followed by the advance of the White f-Pawn.

24 ... Nf8   25 b3 a5   26 f5

White's strategy bears fruit; the exchange of Pawns will now leave him with a passed Pawn on e5 and an open f-file for his Rook. Note how the Bishop on c4 and Pawn on b3 completely neutralize any pressure Black might hope to obtain down the b-file.

26 ... exf5   27 Rxf5 Nh7   28 Rcf1

White avoids the neat trap *28 Rf7 Ng5!* after which Black would gain material.

28 ... Qd8   29 Qg3 Re7   30 h4

Black's squares are gradually being taken away from him. The Knight is not going to be allowed to emerge at g5.

30 ... Rbb7   31 e6 Rbc7

After *31 ... Nf6*, White's attack would break through with *32 Rxf6! gxf6 33 Rxf6 Rh7 34 Qe5 Rbg7* (to prevent the deadly discovered check) *35 Rf7*, with e7 to follow.

32 Qe5 Qe8   33 a4 Qd8   34 R1f2 Qe8   35 R2f3 Qd8 36 Bd3!

After apparently toying with his opponent for a few moves, Fischer seizes upon a winning plan. The decisive attack is to take place on the b1–h7 diagonal, to which Bishop and Queen are now shifted.

36 ... Qe8   37 Qe4

The threat is a forced mate in three moves with *38 Rf8+! Nxf8 39 Rxf8+ Qxf8 40 Qh7 mate*. The Knight must emerge from its hiding place.

37 ... Nf6

38 Rxf6!

The same shattering combination mentioned in the note to move 32. Although Black's Rooks defend the second rank, they cannot counter White's many threats.

38 ... gxf6   39 Rxf6 Kg8   40 Bc4

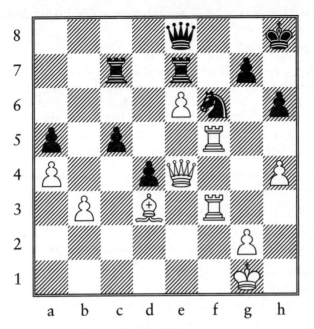

Having done its job on d3, the Bishop returns to its rightful diagonal. The immediate threat is *41 Rf7* beating a path through to the Black King.

40 ... Kh8   41 Qf4   resigns.

The threat is *42 Rf8+ Qxf8   43 Qxf8+ Kh7   44 Bd3 mate*, and *41 ... Kg8   42 Qxh6* leaves Black completely helpless: *42 ... Rcb7   43 Rg6+ Rg7   44 e7+ Qf7   45 Rxg7 mate*.

A beautifully conducted game by Fischer, who never eased up after obtaining a grip on the position.

After defeating Spassky, Fischer, like Morphy more than a century before him, withdrew from active chess. Despite long discussions concerning the match conditions, nothing could induce him to come out and play when the time came for him to defend his title. Accordingly Anatoly Karpov (b. 1951) rose to the World Champion's throne in 1975, the first man to have assumed the crown by default.

After that, Karpov established himself as fully worthy of the title with a series of impressive tournament victories and title defences, particularly against the challenge of Viktor Korchnoi, whose status of Soviet defector once again brought a political slant to the matches. Karpov's win in the final game of the 1978 match was a fine attacking effort.

Game 13: Karpov–Korchnoi, Baguio City 1978 Pirc Defence

1 e4 d6   *2* d4 Nf6   *3* Nc3 g6   *4* Nf3 Bg7   *5* Be2 0-0   *6* 0-0 c5

Black at last challenges the White centre. Rather than exchange Pawns, Karpov advances in the centre to emphasize his advantage in space.

7 d5 Na6

Now that the Pawn formation has clarified, both players can think about their plans for the middlegame. White has more room in the centre, which he would like to increase by playing e5; Black has more room on the Q-side, and would like to advance a Pawn to b5, alongside its colleague at c5. For this reason, Black brings his Knight to c7 via a6. On that square, it will support a later advance of the b-Pawn to b5, while also Black's two Knights and Queen potentially attacking d5 will make White's e5 advance harder to organize.

8 Bf4 Nc7   *9* a4

A necessary precaution. *9* e5 dxe5   *10* Bxe5 Nfxd5 would just have lost White a Pawn, while *9* Re1 would have allowed *9* . . . b5! since *10* Bxb5 Nxb5   *11* Nxb5 Qb6 would quickly regain the Pawn on b2 for Black after the Knight is chased away from b5.

9 . . . b6   *10* Re1 Bb7

Black continues his plan of restraint by pressuring d5. There is no threat to the Pawn itself, but White's e-Pawn must stay at e4 to defend it. Black still wants to play Qd7, a6 and b5 to develop a Q-side initiative.

11 Bc4!

A good move for two reasons: the Bishop gives another support to d5, while also White can now play Qd3 or Qe2 adding to the control of b5 making it harder for Black to carry out his planned advance on the Q-side.

11 ... Nh5 12 Bg5 Nf6

A strange piece of dithering by Black. White quietly continues with his plan.

13 Qd3 a6 14 Rad1 Rb8 15 h3

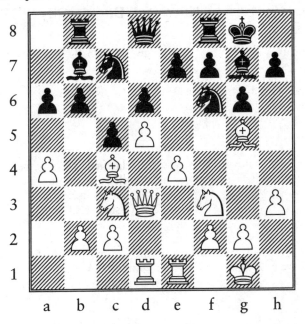

White has developed all his men sensibly and now has enough additional support for the d-Pawn to be able to consider advancing e5. His ultimate plan is to utilize his extra space in the centre for an attack against the Black King. For this reason, he intends to exchange the Bishop on g7 by means of the manoeuvre Qe3 and Bh6. The Pawn is put on h3 to prevent the Queen being molested by Ng4.

15 ... Nd7

The Knight retreats to put an extra guard on e5.

16 Qe3 Ba8 17 Bh6 b5 18 Bxg7 Kxg7 19 Bf1 Nf6
20 axb5 axb5

Both sides have succeeded in their short-term strategic objectives. Black has got his Pawns moving at last; White has exchanged the black-squared Bishops. The task for White now is to create the circumstances under which he can play the planned e5 advance without having to fear the loss of the d-Pawn.

21 Ne2 Bb7   22 Ng3 Ra8   23 c3 Ra4   24 Bd3!

White's regrouping manoeuvre is complete; he has envisaged using Queen, Bishop and both Knights in a powerful attacking combination.

24 ... Qa8

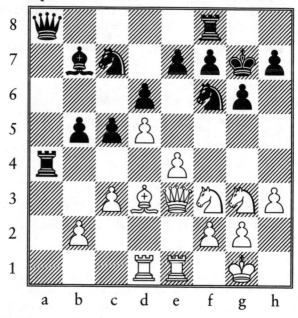

25 e5!

At last it comes, and with great force. White's idea is seen in the following variation: *25 ... Nfxd5   26 Nh5+! gxh5   27 Qg5+ Kh8   28 Qh6 f5* (to prevent Qxh7 mate) *29 Ng5* and White will mate on h7 anyway. Note the role of all White's pieces in this play and the importance of the Bishop on d3 and Knight on g3. It is clear that Karpov had seen this very clearly when playing *21 Ne2*. The last point to notice is that Black cannot decline the sacrifices: after *25 ... Nfxd5   26 Nh5+ Kh8   27 Qh6* the threat is mate on g7, *27 ... gxh5* allows mate on h7, and *27 ... Rg8   28 Ng5* mates next move. Black must capture on e5.

25 ... dxe5   26 Qxe5

Black's position begins to fall apart as c7 and e7 are attacked and the f6 Knight is pinned.

26 ... Nxd5   27 Bxb5 Ra7   28 Nh4

Introducing new attacking combinations with Nf5+.

28 ... Bc8   29 Be2 Be6   30 c4

Finally White cashes in on his attack. The Knight must move and the c5-Pawn will fall. After that, the two passed Pawns on the Q-side should be enough to decide the game.

30 ... Nb4   31 Qxc5 Qb8   32 Bf1 Rc8   33 Qg5 Kh8   34 Rd2

Black is still faced with problems on the K-side. *34 ... Bxc4* would allow *35 Rxe7! Rxe7   36 Qxf6+*.

34 ... Nc6   35 Qh6 Rg8   36 Nf3 Qf8   37 Qe3

White switches from wing to wing in order to stretch the Black defences.

37 ... Kg7   38 Ng5 Bd7   39 b4

The Pawns begin to roll and the end comes nearer. Black cannot capture on b4 without leaving his Rook to be taken by the Queen.

39 ... Qa8   40 b5 Na5   41 b6

Here the first session of the game ended after five hours' play. Black sealed his next move in the envelope provided to ensure secrecy, but his position was so bad that he did not resume the next day. After *41 ... Ra6   42 c5* Black loses his Rook for the Bishop on f1, while *41 ... Rb7   42 Ra2* will quickly win the pinned Knight on a5 after a further Rea1 or Qc3.

In 1985 Garry Kasparov became world champion by defeating Anatoly Karpov. They played in all five closely contested matches for the title, with Kasparov always succeeding in retaining his title. In 1993, however, England's Nigel Short beat Karpov and qualified as the official challenger to Kasparov. However, financial arguments then led to a political schism in the chess world, with Kasparov and Short rejecting the terms offered by the International Chess Federation (FIDE) and forming their own Professional Chess Association (PCA). By the end of 1993, each rival body had organized its own world championship, and the chess world had two champions: Garry Kasparov for the PCA, Anatoly Karpov for FIDE. The next game comes from Kasparov's successful defence of his PCA title.

Game 14: Kasparov–Anand, New York 1995
Ruy Lopez

1 e4 e5   2 Nf3 Nc6   3 Bb5 a6   4 Ba4 Nf6   5 0-0
Nxe4   6 d4 b5   7 Bb3 d5   8 dxe5 Be6   9 Nbd2 Nc5
10 c3 d4   11 Ng5

This extraordinary move was first played in the Karpov–Korchnoi match of 1978. White calmly puts his Knight where Black appears to be able to capture it with impunity. Needless to say, there are some deep tactics involved: after 11 ... Qxg5   12 Qf3! Black has no completely satisfactory way to defend c6. For example 12 ... Bd7   13 Qxf7+ or 12 ... Kd7 13 Bd5.

11 ... dxc3   12 Nxe6 fxe6   13 bxc3 Qd3   14 Bc2!

Kasparov had played 14 Nf3 in an earlier game of the match. This time he was prepared with the results of a good deal of homework.

14 ... Qxc3   15 Nb3!! Nxb3   16 Bxb3

Anand now thought for almost an hour before deciding not to accept the offered Rook in the corner. After 16 ... Qxa1, Kasparov had planned 17 Qh5+ g6 18 Qf3 Nd8 19 Qf6! Rg8   20 Bg5 with a winning attack. If after 17 ... Qh5+ Black plays 17 ... Kd7, then White wins with 18 Bxe6+! Kxe6 19 Qg4+ Kf7   20 Qf3+ Ke6 (20 ... Kg8 allows immediate mate by Qd5) 21 Qxc6+ Bd6   22 exd6 again with a winning attack. Note how in this last line Black's King never dares to tread on a black square for fear of allowing the Bishop to move from c1 with check, discovering an attack by the Rook on Black's Queen.

16 ... Nd4   17 Qg4! Qxa1   18 Bxe6 Rd8

Preventing the very powerful Bd7+, but allowing something just as bad.

19 Bh6!! Qc3   20 Bxg7 Qd3

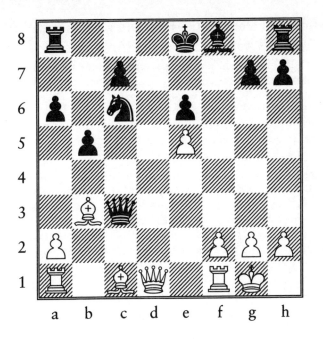

Black would have liked to exchange pieces with *20 . . . Bxg7*, but White does not oblige by recapturing. Instead *21 Qh5+* forces mate next move.

21 Bxh8 Qg6

Until this moment, Kasparov had used only 6 minutes of the 2 hours' thinking time allocated for his first 40 moves. A terrifying example of the potential depth of opening preparation. White now reaches an endgame a Pawn ahead, and his ultimate victory is assured.

22 Bf6 Be7   *23* Bxe7 Qxg4   *24* Bxg4 Kxe7   *25* Rc1 c6
26 f4 a5   *27* Kf2 a4   *28* Ke3 b4   *29* Bd1 a3   *30* g4 Rd5
31 Rc4 c5   *32* Ke4 Rd8   *33* Rxc5 Ne6   *34* Rd5 Rc8
35 f5 Rc4+   *36* Ke3 Nc5   *37* g5 Rc1   *38* Rd6   resigns.

The finish would have been *38 . . .* b3   *39* f6+ Kf8   *40* e6! Nxe6   *41* Bxb3 Nxg5   *42* Rd8 mate.

Game 15: Deep Blue–Kasparov, Philadelphia 1996
Sicilian Defence

In 1996, the world's strongest chess player faced the world's most powerful chess computer in a challenge match. 'Deep Blue' was a project that had begun in the 1970s as a chess program called Deep Thought which became the first to win a tournament ahead of human Grandmasters. In 1990, its programmers were recruited by IBM for a mission with the stated aim of defeating the world champion.

Making a billion calculations and looking at up to a hundred million chess positions every second, Deep Blue was clearly a formidable opponent. Kasparov had lost to computers before, but only in quick-play games where fast time-limits created greater hazards for human fallibility. This match, however, was at the normal tournament rate which allocated each player 2 hours for 40 moves. When Kasparov was beaten in the opening game, it was the first time a machine had beaten the world champion under such conditions.

Kasparov eventually won the match by three wins to one with two draws, after correctly diagnosing certain areas of definite weakness in the computer's chess understanding. When the position is not susceptible to direct calculation – when there are no capturing sequences or checks or similar forcing moves available – even a monster such as Deep Blue is liable to enter a planless dither and let its opponent systematically improve his position unopposed. But when the game comes down to a direct tactical confrontation, the machine is master, as the opening game showed.

1 e4 c5   2 c3 d5   3 exd5 Qxd5   4 d4 Nf6   5 Nf3 Bg4
6 Be2 e6   7 h3 Bh5   8 0-0 Nc6   9 Be3 cxd4   10
cxd4 Bb4   11 a3 Ba5   12 Nc3 Qd6

The position is one of a type of dynamic equilibrium common in top-class chess. The Pawn on d4 controls c5 and e5, either of which could be an important outpost in a future White attack. By comparison, the Black Pawn on e6 has a primarily defensive function. The Pawn on d4, however, is isolated and may become vulnerable later in the game.

13 Nb5

A very machine-like move. Most strong human players would not be tempted by this attack on the Queen. White may gain a move now by forcing the Queen to move, but the Knight will almost certainly be forced back in a move or two when Black plays . . . a6 and the whole manoeuvre will end up losing time. On this occasion, however, the machine proves to be correct.

**13 . . . Qe7   14 Ne5 Bxe2   15 Qxe2 0-0   16 Rac1 Rac8
17 Bg5! Bb6   18 Bxf6 gxf6**

Recapturing with the Queen would have allowed a Knight fork on d7.

19 Nc4 Rfd8

And here, *19 . . . Bxd4   20 Nxd4 Nxd4* runs into a Queen fork with *21 Qg4+*.

**20 Nxb6 axb6   21 Rfd1 f5   22 Qe3 Qf6   23 d5! Rxd5
24 Rxd5 exd5   25 b3!**

Calmly safeguarding its b-Pawn, Deep Blue knows that it will regain the Pawn on b6, leaving Black with many weak Pawns. Note that *25 . . . d4* is simply met by *26 Nxd4*, exploiting the pin along the c-file.

**25 . . . Kh8   26 Qxb6 Rg8   27 Qc5 d4   28 Nd6 f4
29 Nxb7 Ne5   30 Qd5 f3   31 g3 Nd3   32 Rc7 Re8
33 Nd6 Re1+   34 Kh2 Nxf2**

Given one more move, Black could deliver checkmate with Rh1. Sadly, he never gets the chance.

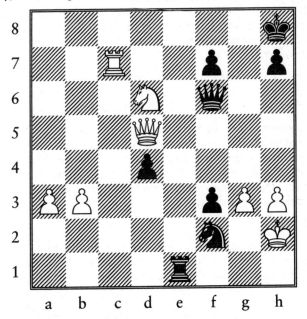

35 Nxf7+ Kg7

Black could try 35 Qxf7, hoping for 36 Qxf7? Rh1 mate, but White plays instead 37 Qd8+! winning easily after either 37 ... Re8   38 Qxd4+ or 37 ... Qg8   38 Qf6+.

36 Ng5+ Kh6   37 Rxh7+   Black resigned.

After 37 . . . Kg6 there follows 38 Qg8+ Kf5   39 Nxf3, stopping Black's mate threat and leaving White three Pawns up with a winning attack.

In 1998, an improved, and even faster version of Deep Blue defeated Kasparov in a new match, with three wins, one loss and two draws from their six games. Having achieved their ambition, IBM declined Kasparov's challenge to a return match saying that Deep Blue had better things to do with its time than play chess.

Four years later, man's intellectual battle against silicon took a further step backwards when Kasparov's successor as World Champion, Vladimir Kramnik, challenged a program called Deep Fritz to a six-game match. Unlike Deep Blue, which was a dedicated mainframe computer that could calculate more than a billion chess positions every second, Fritz was an ordinary CD-Rom run on a PC that calculated at around a million positions every second. All the same, the match ended tied at 3-3, delivering another bruise to the human ego.

09

the art of chess compositions

In this chapter you will learn:
- how to compose and solve chess problems, studies and puzzles.

Chess problems and studies

Until now, the subject matter of this book has been concerned with the practical task of playing the game of chess: how to recognize and create advantages, how to defend disadvantageous positions, how to win good positions, how to save bad ones. But there is another side to chess, which exploits the geometric beauty inherent in the game, without the crude competitiveness needed when two people play against one another. The world of the chess problem is the domain of the chess artist. His positions are not arrived at by two antagonists working in competition, but by one composer seeking to illustrate an attractive chess idea. If at the same time he can tantalize the solver, then his task has fully succeeded.

The types of chess composition are many and highly varied, ranging from the endgame study, where the task of the solver is closest to that of the normal player – to win or draw from the position given – to the far reaches of 'fairy chess' where the whole object of the game may be reversed and even the moves of the pieces changed in order to illustrate a beautiful idea. In the following pages, several different types of problem are illustrated. You might like to try to find the solutions yourself, but in many cases simply playing through the moves of the solution is an adequate way to appreciate the beauty of the composer's intention.

Strictly speaking, the term 'chess problem' is normally reserved for a composed position in which the side to play (conventionally White) is stipulated to force mate within a given number of moves.

Opposite is an example of a Mate in Two Moves problem by W. Speckman.

White has any number of ways of forcing mate in *three* moves; for example *1* Kxf6+ Kf8 *2* Qg7+ Ke8 *3* Qe7 mate, or *1* Rc8+ Kf8 *2* Rxd8+ Ke7 *3* Qd6 mate. But the conditions of the task demand a mate in two. The only way to solve it involves a change in direction by the Queen and a delayed use of the discovered check: *1* **Qb8! Rxb8** *2* **Rc8 mate.** The sacrifice of the Queen sets up the double check and mate on the next move. After *1* Qb8, Black has no escape; the threat is *2* Qxd8 mate, and *1* ... Rf8 allows *2* Rh4 mate.

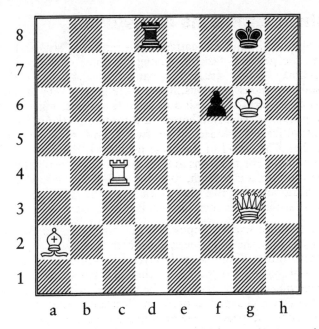

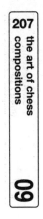

Such a problem appeals to the player of the game because of the sacrificial idea in the solution and the elegance of expression of the idea on the board. The next example, however, is a pure problemist's problem, of elaborate construction and great richness in the mating variations.

Attention in the position on page 208 is focused on the four directions in which discovered checks can be unleashed: the diagonals c1–f4, b8–f4, e2–a6 and along the rank a4–f4. At the moment, any discovered check by moving the Rook from e3 would allow the Black King to escape to g3 or e5, while any check delivered by moving the Knight from d6 would be met by the capture of the Pawn on f5. The solution is *1 Be4!*, defending the Pawn on f5 and threatening *2 Nxc4* mate. The surprising point of the move is that it unpins the Knight on c4 and lets Black deliver his own discovered checks.

As we shall see, the composer has catered for everything: after *1 Be4*, *1 . . . Nb6* (or Na5 or Na3 or Nb2) are still met by *2 Nc4* mate. Each of the other Knight checks has its own mate ready in answer: *1 . . . Nxd6+ 2 Bd3* mate; or *1 . . . Ne5+ 2 Rd3* mate; or *1 . . . Nxe3+ 2 Nb5* mate; or *1 . . . Nd2+ 2 Nc4* mate. Finally, *1 . . . Ke5 2 Nxc4* is still mate.

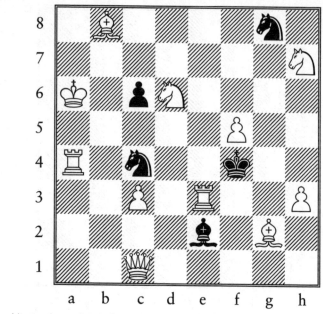

white to play and mate in two moves (by Comins Mansfield)

Before leaving this remarkable composition, it is worth while examining the roles of some of the other pieces which do not take part in the mating variations. One of a problemist's primary concerns is the elimination of possible alternative solutions. (Such unwanted answers spoil a problem and are known as 'cooks'.) In this example the Pawn at c6 and the Knight at g8 are both there just in order to eliminate other crude mates in two. For example, without the Pawn on c6, *1 Rd3+ Ke5 2 Rd5* would be mate, while the absence of the Knight from g8 would allow *1 Nc8+ Kxf5 2 Ne7* mate. Lastly, the tempting try *1 Qd1* (threatening *2 Qd4* mate) is met not by *1 ... Bxd1* (*2 Rxc4*) or *1 ... Kxe3* (*2 Qd4*) but by either *1 ... c5* or *1 ... Nf6* when White has no mate.

From a difficult two-mover, here is a comparatively easy three-mover:

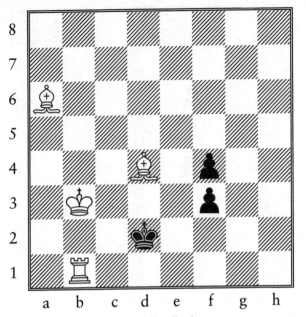

white to play and mate in three (by V. Korolkov)

Again the task of winning the game is not difficult, but the three-move stipulation makes a problem of it. The only solution is *1 Re1!* Kxe1 (otherwise *2 Bc3* is mate) *2 Kc2* f2 (Black has no other move) *3 Bc3* mate. This is another problem to delight players through the surprise of the key-move *1 Re1*, but is liable to be seen as rather trivial by the dedicated problemist.

Problems of the mate-in-two or mate-in-three type are the most commonly encountered compositions, but one occasionally meets four-movers, five-movers or even longer problems. The difficulty with such longer problems is to retain some interest in the play while ensuring soundness and an absence of further solutions.

The position on page 210 is a pathological monstrosity, showing just how far some composers are prepared to go.

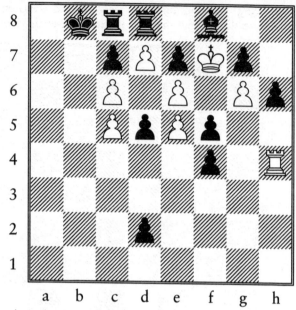

white to play and mate in 102 moves (by Dr O. T. Blathy)

The solution opens with the moves *1 Rh1 Ka7 2 Ra1+ Kb8*, and now White's plan is to force Black to run out of Pawn moves, after which he will have to play either Re8 or Rxd7. So: *3 Kg8 Re8 4 Kh8 Red8 5 Kh7 Rc8 6 Kg8 Red8 7 Kf7*. White has lost a move by his King's triangulation over the square h8, so now Black must advance a Pawn, for example by *7 . . . h5*. Then the same thing happens again: *8 Kg8 Re8 9 Kh8* and so on, with Black forced to move a Pawn every five moves. Eventually (it works out at move 57) one of the Pawns must promote: *57 . . . d1=Q 58 Rxd1 Ka7 59 Ra1+ Kb8 60 Kg8* and round we go again. By move 96, Black has run out of Pawns, with White having captured the last newly promoted piece on that move. The solution then ends: *96 . . . Ka7 97 Ra1+ Kb8 98 Ra2 Rxd7 99 exd7 Rd8 100 e6 Rc8 101 dxc8=Q+ Kxc8 102 Ra8 mate*.

Moving on from the world of problems, we come to the endgame study. In this area of chess composition, the task is not to win in a specified number of moves but, more normal to the player, just to win (or to save the game in some cases). Some endgame studies are actually pieces of technique which might reasonably be thought to have arisen in an actual game.

The following position appears realistic and innocent, but despite the small material the play is extraordinarily rich:

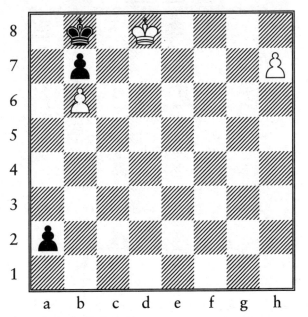

white to play and win (by D. Joseph)

The first move is easy, *1 h8=Q*. Black's defence should also not be hard to see: *1 . . . a1=Q!*. Now *2 Qxa1?* would be stalemate. The correct way to continue is *2 Qg8! Qa2!* (again the only defence to the threat of a killing discovered check by the White King) *3 Qe8! Qa4! 4 Qe5+ Ka8 5 Qh8!* and White wins, since Black can no longer oppose Queens without his being taken with check.

The precision of the White Queen moves in this endgame is very important. After *1 h8=Q a1=Q* it would be a mistake to play immediately *2 Qe8?* because Black would then be able to defend with *2 . . . Qg7!* and prevent White's King from emerging. Equally, *2 Qf8?* would be a mistake since after *2 . . . Qa3! 3 Qe8* Black has the defence *3 . . . Qd6+*, again saving the game.

The precision of play in this study combined with the surprise element of the stalemate defences is a good example of what the composer strives after when trying to create such an endgame.

The next example is from the wilder excesses of the imagination:

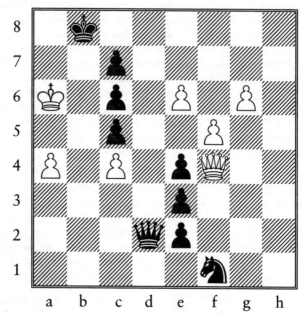

white to play and draw (by V. Korolkov and L. Mitrofanov)

The two sets of tripled Pawns make the position look quite ungamelike, but their presence is justified by the extravagance of the idea which they contain. Here is the solution, which is one of the best examples of chessboard humour ever devised:

1 Qe5 (threatens Qh8 mate) **Qa5+!** *2 Kxa5 Kb7!* *3 Qb2+ Ka7* *4 Qb8+!* (*4 Qxe2 Nd2!* would leave White helpless against mate on c4 or b3). *4 ... Kxb8* *5 Ka6!* **e1=Q** *6 g7!* Qa5+ (*6 ... Qg3* *7 e7* would win for White) *7 Kxa5 Kb7* *8 g8=Q e2* *9 Qa8+!* Kxa8 *10 Ka6 e1=Q* *11 e7 Qa5+* *12 Kxa5 Kb7* *13 e8=Q Nd2* *14 Qa8+!* Kxa8 *15 Ka6* Nxc4 (both sides have run out of Queens to sacrifice and the solution drifts to a peaceful close) *16 f6 Ne5* *17 f7!* Nd7 *18 f8=Q+!* Nxf8 *19 a5* and whatever Black plays White is stalemated. A magnificent concoction (but easy once you get the right idea!).

Fantasy in chess composition

In the realms of both problems and endgame studies, however wild and unlikely the position, the game is still chess. There are, however, certain types of problem where the rules of the game are bent a little in order to illustrate other facets of the chess pieces. There is the *self-mate*, in which White's object is not to mate his opponent, but to force Black to mate him. More conspiratorial is the *helpmate* in which both sides' moves endeavour to reach the same objective – a mate for White. These are both deviant versions known under the general heading of Fairy Chess, which may be extended to include practically anything which can go on on a chessboard.

A personal favourite of the author is the *series helpmate*, in which Black makes a set number of moves, without White moving at all, then White gives mate in one move. The only further stipulation is that Black must not give check on any of his moves before the last one. It is important, if the problem is to be considered a good one, that the solution should be unique even to the order in which the Black moves must be played. The next two diagrams form an amusing and tantalizing pair:

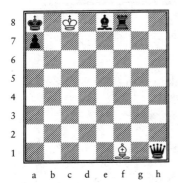

Black makes six consecutive moves to allow White to deliver mate in one.

The difficulty lies in where to hide the Black pieces so that they cannot interpose after White's mating move. (The solution is given after the next position.)

series helpmate in six
(by N. A. Macleod)

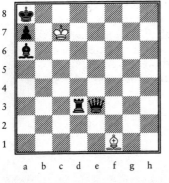

One move shorter than the previous position, but Black's five moves are more difficult to find.

series helpmate in five
(by N. A. Macleod)

The solutions to these two problems are in fact so different from one another that solving the first can be positively detrimental to one's ability to find the answer to the second.

In the first position, the mating move will be the obvious Bg2; the only squares on which to hide the Queen and Rook are a1 and h1 respectively, and the Black Bishop will have to be captured on g2. The only way all this can be achieved within the six moves is: 1 Qh8, 2 Qa1, 3 Rh8, 4 Rh1, 5 Bc6, 6 Bg2 and White finally plays Bxg2 mate. The fact that Queen and Rook both utilize h1 and h8 in this sequence, and that the Bishop cannot move from e8 until the Rook is off the back rank (otherwise the White King would be in check), make the order of moves unique.

Searching for a similar mating position within the five moves stipulated for the second position would prove unavailing. The solution this time is 1 Bb7, 2 a5, 3 Ka7, 4 Ka6, 5 Qa7 and now White mates with Bxd3. Again note the neat mechanism which forces the black pieces to adopt a unique move order: the Bishop must move first to allow the Pawn to advance, then the King must traverse a7 before the Queen can occupy that square.

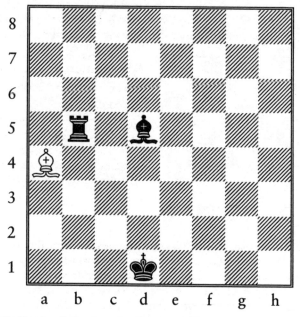

the White King is missing from the diagram position
where should it be? (composed by Raymond Smullyan)

And one final example before leaving the rarefied atmosphere of chess fantasy. Our last position is an exercise in *retro-analysis*, where the task is not to determine the next moves in the position, but to establish its past history.

This is an exercise in chessboard logic. The difficulty arises from the fact that the Black King appears to be in check from the White Bishop. (Indeed, he is in check, unless the White King stands on b3.) But how did the Bishop move to a4, if indeed it has just delivered check on that square? Not along the e8–a4 diagonal, for the Black Rook would have been in the way. Neither from c2 or b3, since Black would already have been in check. So is White's King on b3? Unfortunately, that too is impossible, since it would be in double check from Rook and Bishop in an impossible manner. (Neither black checking piece could have just moved to discover check from the other.) The only possible solution is that White's King has just moved from b3, discovering check from the White Bishop. And there is only one way this could have come about without having been preceded by that same illegal double check.

To see the solution, we need to add a Black Pawn on b4 and a White Pawn on c2. Now place the White King on b3, giving the position below. Black has just moved his Bishop to give check at d5. White replies *1* c4 and the Pawn is taken en passant:

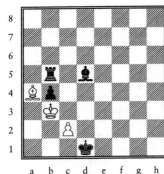

1 c4   bxc3 e.p.

The apparently illegal double check is on the board!

2 Kxc3

and the problem is solved. This is indeed the only way the first position could have been reached, so the answer is that the White King is on c3.

That, of course, has strayed a long way from real chess, but I hope that this brief excursion into the world of chess problems and compositions will encourage some readers to explore more of the fringes of chess, where there is as much beauty to be found as in the more competitive world of the chess tournament.

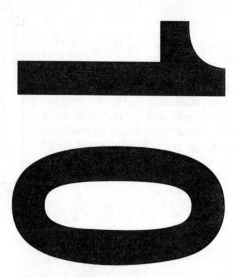

10
chess in the twenty-first century

What next?

So now you know how the pieces move, you are acquainted with the basic tactics of the game, and you understand a little of how strategic plans are formulated and carried out. You should now know enough to play through the moves of a top-class game and, even if you will not understand the full reasons behind many of the moves, you should still be able to form a good picture of what the players were trying to accomplish and how each move fitted into a grand plan. But in chess as in almost every other art or game, there is a huge difference between the ability to appreciate a good performance and the ability to deliver one.

That leaves us with the most difficult question of all: how do I improve my game? The standard answer is simply to keep playing, to seek out opponents a little stronger than yourself, and to play through the games of the masters in newspaper chess columns and books. A chess computer, or a chess program for a personal computer, can be a great asset, especially as most of these now allow the human player to choose an appropriate level of strength to play against. The market leader Fritz, for example, recently tied a match against the world's strongest player, yet allows the home user to dampen its strength down to near beginner's level.

Many dedicated chess computers offer attractive design features such as touch-sensitive boards, which recognize when a move is played and allow a game to be conducted almost as though playing against a human. Some even incorporate electromagnetic circuitry that allows them to move their own pieces. In general, however, programs for home computers provide far better value for money in terms of both playing strength and the range of options offered.

The best advice I can offer on selecting a chess computer is to try it out before buying. Do not be seduced by information on the packet. You need to be sure that it is strong enough to give you a good game, and that its mode of operation is user-friendly. If you beat it the first time you play, you can be sure it will not be very useful for long. And if you find yourself cursing at the fiddly nature of its operation, it will surely soon be left to rust on the shelf.

Chess on the Internet is another recent development that is growing hugely in popularity. Indeed, you only need to enter 'chess' into any Internet search engine to discover the bewilderingly vast range of possibilities. Chess lessons, chess news, downloadable chess programs, databases of historic games, live coverage of current international tournaments, and the possibility to play a competitive game with someone on another continent are all just a few mouse clicks away.

If you are simply looking for a game, the top of the range is the Internet Chess Club (ICC) that you will find at **www.chessclub.com**. At any given moment, around a thousand players, from casual club player to Grandmaster, are usually to be found doing battle online, so it does not take long to find an opponent of the right strength. A similar service can be found at **www.kasparovchess.com**, the former world champion's chess club website, which also offers a full range of other chess information and advice. Both the ICC and Kasparov Chess are subscription sites, but non-members can log in as guests, or take advantage of free trial offers.

You can also find an opponent on various free sites, such as the games section of **yahoo.com**, or a dedicated chess site such as **www.chess.net**. Unsurprisingly, these are less well organized and often more haphazard than the subscription sites.

Another good starting place is the home page of Chess magazine: **www.chess.co.uk**, which is not only a commercial site for the sale of chess goods, but also provides a home for the marvellous online chess news service 'The Week In Chess' (www.chess.co.uk/twic/twic.html). This offers up-to-date news and games from current events, as well as links to tournament sites.

All the above sites offer links to similar ones, so wherever you start, you will probably soon find yourself thick in the jungle of Internet chess. But will it help you play better? As I said, the best way to improve is by practice against a stronger player, but playing through the games of the great masters can be an excellent substitute. It is, after all, less painful to learn from other people's mistakes than from your own, and that brings us to the topic of chess books.

It used to be said that there were more books on chess than on all other games combined. I do not know if that was ever true, but there are certainly a vast number, with more and more being published every week. There is certainly no better way to develop an understanding of the finer points of the game than by having a good teacher explain what is going on in a well-played game, but with so many books on the market, there are many pot-boilers and only few true classics.

I can unhesitatingly recommend three books written in the 1920s that still give a marvellous grasp of the essentials of chess strategy. These are *My System* by A. Nimzowitsch, and *Masters of the Chessboard* and *Modern Ideas in Chess*, both by R. Reti. The books by Reti are particularly perceptive and beautifully written. For a more modern approach, David Bronstein's *The Modern Chess Self-Tutor* is full of instructive and entertaining examples of Grandmasterly thought processes. Or if you have enjoyed this book, you might find *Teach Yourself Better Chess* as good a way as any to move forward.

I have not yet mentioned any of the numerous monographs on individual opening variations. These, on the whole, are I think best avoided, as they add little to general chess understanding while giving a vast amount of specialized detail. The games collections of the great players are a better way to acquire a feel for the way a game develops from opening through middlegame to endgame.

The game of chess has lasted for generations of Grandmasters and beginners and still looks as full of life as ever. Played for fun or in deadly earnest, it continues to bring great pleasure to its addicts.

When played between friends at home, players chat over their moves, and even let each other take back mistakes. But in serious games, moves are never retracted, and there is even a rule specifying that a piece once touched must be moved, if possible. For anyone planning to become a serious player at any level, the habit of 'touch–move' is an important one to acquire as soon as possible. Whatever the level of chess, the rules specify that once the hand has quitted the piece being moved, that move must stand and may not be retracted.

In serious chess, too, the game is played with clocks timing each player's moves, the regulations specifying that a certain number of moves must be made within a specified time. The penalty for overstepping the time limit is immediate forfeit of the game. The habit of playing with clocks is another which it is best to acquire as soon as possible in one's chess life.

Chess is played as an organized sport in practically every country, with tournaments arranged for players of every standard. Club champions may aspire to play for their counties;

county champions may qualify for the national championship. National champions may compete in the laborious series of tournaments which qualify for the world championship itself. Whatever level you finally reach, I hope this small work will have helped encourage you to participate, as player or even just interested spectator, in the world of chess.

Forms of chess notation

Throughout this book, we have used the simplest and most concise form of chess notation, the so-called 'short algebraic' system. This is gradually becoming adopted as the only universally accepted form of notation for chess moves, but other systems are also still encountered, particularly in English-speaking countries, where the old 'Descriptive Notation' is dying a lingering death. While learning the game, it is best to stick to a single method of writing down the moves, but for full enjoyment of the widest possible range of chess literature, it is necessary to be familiar with other systems. Here is a summary of the three most commonly encountered notations.

Short Algebraic As used in this book: the files are identified by the letters a–h, the ranks 1–8 (counting from White's side). Each square has a unique alpha-numeric coordinate, the moves being indicated in general by the initial letter of the piece moved (K, Q, R, N, B, nothing for Pawn) and the square of arrival. In the case of ambiguity, an extra symbol is added to remove the confusion. Captures are indicated by 'x', check by '+'.

Full Algebraic As in short algebraic, except that the square of departure of the moving piece is also included in the move description. Thus the opening moves *1* d4 Nf6 become, in the full form, *1* d2–d4 Ng8–f6.

Descriptive Notation There are two principal differences between this and the algebraic forms of notation. Firstly, the files are known not by the letters a–h, but by the names of the pieces which occupy them at the start of the game. The a-file becomes the QR-file (Queen's Rook file), the b-file is the QN-file (Queen's Knight's file), and so on through the QB, Q, K, KB, and KN-files, finally reaching the KR-file. The second main difference is that each square has not one but two descriptions, depending on whether it is viewed from Black's or White's side of the board. The square e1 is known as K1 to White but K8 to Black (the eighth square on the K-file from Black's point of view). White's moves are written down as viewed by White, Black's moves as seen by Black. Thus the opening moves *1* d4 Nf6 become *1* P–Q4 N–KB3 (note the added dignity of a P for Pawn and the insertion of '–' between the piece and its destination). In case of ambiguity, a distinction may be made between pieces which started the game on the K-side and those which started on the Q-side of the board; thus, after *1* P–Q4 N–KB3 *2* N–KB3 P–K3 (*1* d4 Nf6 *2* Nf3 e6) the move *3* Nbd2 would be written *3* QN–Q2 (the Queen's Knight moves to Q2). Even if pieces change places during the course of a game, they remain the QN or the QR, though they may stand on the K-side of the board. If confusion is liable to arise, the move might be written as N(N1)–Q2. In the interests of brevity, it is sufficient to write N1 (meaning QN1 rather than KN1) if no ambiguity arises.

A simple game in all three notations should clarify the differences:

Short algebraic		*Full algebraic*		*Descriptive*	
1 e4	e5	1 e2–e4	e7–e5	1 P–K4	P–K4
2 Bc4	d6	2 Bf1–c4	d7–d6	2 B–B4	P–Q3
3 Nf3	Nc6	3 Ng1–f3	Nb8–c6	3 N–KB3	N–QB3
4 Nc3	Bg4	4 Nb1–c3	Bc8–g4	4 N–B3	B–N5
5 h3	Bh5	5 h2–h3	Bg4–h5	5 P–KR3	B–R4
6 d3	h6	6 d2–d3	h7–h6	6 P–Q3	P–KR3
7 Nxe5	Bxd1	7 Nf3xe5	Bh5xd1	7 NxP	BxQ
8 Bxf7+	Ke7	8 Bc4xf7+	Ke8–e7	8 BxPch	K–K2
9 Nd5 mate.		9 Nc3–d5 mate.		9 N–Q5 mate.	

Note the practice in descriptive notation of naming the captured piece rather than the square upon which the capture takes place. This is the only facet of descriptive notation which is more economical than the algebraic system – even the 'ch' for check utilizes an extra symbol.

backward pawn   A Pawn that has fallen behind its colleagues on the two neighbouring files, leaving weak squares or holes in front of it.

bad bishop   A Bishop whose effectiveness is limited by its own pPawns on the same colour squares.

castling   The special double-move of King and Rook allowed only once in the game by each player.

centre   The squares d4, e4, d5 and e5; much of the early battle in the game is over control of the centre.

check   A threat to capture the King.

checkmate   A threat to capture the King which cannot be met.

closed game   Any opening beginning with the moves 1 d4 d5.

combination   A sequence of moves involving more than once piece that leads to strategic or tactical gains.

development   Getting one's pieces out in the opening, and placing them on effective squares.

diagonal   A line of squares of the same colour, connected at the corners only.

discovered attack   Moving one piece to reveal an attack by another.

doubled pawns   Two Pawns of the same colour on the same file; doubled Pawns may occur only after one of the Pawns has made a capture.

draw by agreement The conclusion of a game when one player offers his opponent a draw and the other accepts; a draw by agreement may be in a sterile position which neither could conceivably win, or through mutual respect in an unclear position.

draw by repetition If the same position occurs three times in the course of the game with the same player to move (usually simply by both players moving a single piece backwards and forwards) a draw by repetition may be claimed.

en passant A type of capture permitted only by a Pawn, and only under special conditions.

endgame The final phase of the game, when only a few men remain on the board and the Kings may play a full part in the battle.

fianchetto The development of a White Bishop on g2 or b2, or a Black one on g7 or b7.

fifty-move rule If both sides have made 50 moves without moving a Pawn or making a capture, then the player whose turn it is to move may claim a draw.

file A line of squares running up and down the board from White's side to Black's.

flank opening Any opening that begins with a move other than 1 e4 or 1 d4.

fool's mate The shortest possible game, ending with White checkmated after two moves.

fork A simultaneous attack by the same man on two or more enemy pieces.

half-open file A file containing a Pawn or Pawns of one colour only.

hole A square on one player's third or fourth rank that may never be controlled by one of his Pawns.

initiative The ability to dictate the course of the game for several moves through threats and captures.

isolated pawn A Pawn that has no colleagues on either of the neighbouring files; an isolated Pawn is thus deprived of the possibility of protection by another Pawn.

Kriegspiel A chess variant in which each player does not know the location of his opponent's pieces.

material The pieces that remain on the board; material is one of the three main components involved in evaluating a position. (See also 'initiative' and 'space'.)

middlegame The complex period of the game between the opening and endgame.

open file A file with no Pawns of either colour in it.

open game Any opening beginning with moves *1* e4 e5.

opening The earliest phase of the game in which both sides develop their men and plan their later strategies.

overloading When one piece is called upon to perform too many duties simultaneously.

passed pawn A Pawn that has an enemy Pawn, either on its own file or a neighbouring one, impeding its progress to the queening square.

pawn majority Having more Pawns than your opponent in a particular area of the board; a Pawn majority often leads to the creation of a passed Pawn.

perpetual check A form of draw by repetition in which one player forces the draw by giving an endless series of checks to the enemy King.

Philidor's legacy A particular type of combination leading to smothered mate.

pin The immobilization of an enemy piece by forcing it to shield a piece of higher value.

problem A composed position in which White is required to force checkmate within a specified number of moves.

rank A row of squares running horizontally across the board.

sacrifice The deliberate surrender of material in order to make compensatory tactical or strategic gains.

scholar's mate A four-move game that forms the most popular opening trap among beginners.

semi-closed game Any opening beginning *1* d4 in which Black refrains from the reply *1* . . . d5.

semi-open game Any opening beginning *1* e4 in which Black refrains from the reply *1* . . . e5.

smothered mate   A checkmate in which the mated king is hampered by his own pieces; the piece delivering the mate is most often a Knight.

space   The territory controlled by one side; space is one of the principal components used in evaluation of any position.

stalemate   A type of draw that occurs when the player whose turn it is to move is not in check, but has no possible move that does not leave him in check.

strategy   A player's long-term and medium-term objectives.

study   A composed position in which the solver's task is to find a win for White, or a draw, as specified by the composer.

tactics   The hand-to-hand fighting on the chessboard; the threats, captures and other forcing variations that comprise the brief, calculable skirmishes that may occur from a given position.

undermining   Weakening an opponent's defences by attacking enemy pieces and forcing them away from important defensive tasks.

weak square   *See* 'hole'.

zugzwang   A situation in which the compulsion to make a move results in the worsening of one's position.

index